Solitude

The Art of Living with Yourself

Solitude

The Art of Living with Yourself

John Selby

$\mathcal{H}$EARTSFIRE $\mathcal{B}$OOKS

Library of Congress Cataloging-in-Publication Data

Selby, John.
      Solitude: the art of living with yourself/byJohn Selby.— 1st
      ed.
        p. cm.
      ISBN 1-889797-19-7 (ppk) : $12.95

      1. Solitude.   2. Loneliness.   3. Self-acceptance.   4. Interpersonal
      relationships.   5. Self-help techniques.   I. Title
BF575.L7S45   1998   98–212649
155.9'2—DC21   CIP

Cover design by Cisneros Design
Book design and text composition by John Cole GRAPHIC DESIGNER
Printed in the U.S.A.
Text is set in Adobe Minion

First edition 1998
10 9 8 7 6 5 4 3 2 1

Heartsfire Books: 800.988.5170
500 N. Guadalupe Street, Suite G465
Santa Fe, New Mexico 87501 USA

Email: heartsfirebooks@heartsfirebooks.com
Visit us at http://www.heartsfirebooks.com

If you are unable to order this book from your local bookseller, you may order directly from the publisher. Quantity discounts for organizations are available.

CONTENTS

Introduction: Finding Yourself Alone 1

Chapter 1: Learning to Encounter Your
Solitary Self 12

Chapter 2: Exploring and Healing
Loneliness 26

Chapter 3: Becoming Your Own
Best Friend 40
PART I: First Steps 40

Chapter 4: Becoming Your Own
Best Friend 57
PART II: Self-Acceptance 57

Chapter 5: Moving Beyond Loss
and Abandonment 70

Chapter 6: Reviewing Your Life Patterns 82

Chapter 7: Balancing Your New Life 89

Chapter 8: Developing Your Spiritual
Awareness .109

Chapter 9: Finding Happiness in Solitude:
Three Personal Stories 125

Afterword: Preserving Solitary Space 132

Finding Yourself Alone

"I never found a companion that was so companionable as solitude."—Henry David Thoreau

It is one of the most curious paradoxes in human life that we are, at the same time, 100 percent social animals and also completely solitary beings. At certain levels, we are able to share our thoughts and feelings with other people, but on many dimensions our innermost realms of insight, emotion, memories, and dreams remain known only to ourselves.

Human beings require regular periods of solitude for the personality to fully mature. It is extremely important that we develop our relationship with the solitary dimension of our lives, that we come to grips with the challenge of living alone with our own internal selves, and that we become our own best friend in life.

I have observed over and over again in my therapy work that people who are having the most difficulty in establishing meaningful relationships are the same people who are having difficulty in becoming their own best friend. And to the extent that these people learn to love themselves in moments of solitude, they learn how to reach out and love others as well. By learning to love solitude, we learn how to share our inner realms of being more fully with those around us.

This book is designed to help you learn how to relate more deeply, more intimately, more enjoyably with your own self. Especially if you are presently in a stage or period in your life when you are spending considerable time alone, or are unsatisfied with your present levels of interacting with family and friends, then the time is ripe to take an honest look at your existing relationship with yourself and to see how you can enhance that primal relationship. Throughout the book, I will be offering you frequent opportunities to stop reading and explore your memories, habits, and current experience in relation to solitude and your relationship with yourself.

We are, of course, always forced to live with ourselves. We can live completely alone or even retreat from the world entirely, but we are still living with our own personality, no matter what we do. So the essential challenge in all our lives, regardless of our social habits, is to master the fine art of developing a healthy, expanding relationship with ourselves. Then, and only then, can we live life fully and, in addition, become capable of the satisfying involvements we might hunger for with others.

The most lonely, frustrated people I have worked with in my practice have not been the loners, but people who are addicted to social interaction. Afraid to encounter themselves in solitude, they constantly fill their lives with shallow social interactions that keep them from ever finally coming face to face with their own solitary spirit.

It is tragic that with all the education we receive as children these days, we are very seldom taught the basic skills for developing a deep, enduring, intimate relationship with ourselves. Instead, most of us grow up conditioned to fear solitude and develop the habit of avoiding encounters with our inner spirit.

What I hope to do in this book is to guide you through a deep exploration of your relationship with your inner self, so that you can face your apprehensions and learn to know yourself. I hope that, in using this opportunity, you will emerge from the adventure a more complete person, with a full appreciation of who you are, and with the ability to form deeper relationships whenever you feel the desire to expand the social dimension of your life.

In working with the processes in this book, it is important to set aside times each day when you are in fact alone with yourself. This means not only being alone in terms of social interaction, but also free of social extensions such as radio and television, reading material, and other contacts with the thoughts and feelings of other human beings. The first step in developing your relationship, then, is to allow yourself actually to experience being alone, to become aware of your solitary presence.

The second step is learning to recognize how you actually feel about yourself. This is not always easy, because in order to function, almost everyone covers up negative self-judgments to some degree, or denies them altogether. They may appear as a kind of background tape, not noticed; or they may appear as a natural, even virtuous, aspect of our personality—since social conditioning tells us that it is wrong to carry around exaggerated notions of our own worth. To recognize negative patterns of self-judgment, you need to observe your mental habits. Do you in actuality like yourself—even with your faults? Or do you feel bad about who you are? Notice whether you somehow chronically put yourself down, discount yourself, deny your self-worth in countless, small ways. Often, these habits are so subtle and unconscious that you may need to ask another person to notice whether your speech and actions reveal negative self-judgments. In exploring your self-relationship, you need to know how and in what ways you are good friends with yourself, and how in other ways you may be your own worst enemy.

Early in life, we pick up primal conditioning from our parents and extended family regarding how a person should relate to himself or herself. Throughout this book, I will be suggesting at times that you look back to your own childhood and look at how you learned to relate to yourself. You will also need to look at how your parents each related to their own selves and how that affected your experience of being alone and your attitudes toward solitude. Did you learn positive ways of spending time alone? Or did you learn to reject solitary experiences, to fear being alone?

Looking back into the origins of your present habits is an important step in transforming them. But there is also a vital need for much present-moment reflecting, in which you observe your habits in action right now, and come to see how you might be sabotaging your relationship with yourself in the present moments of your life. It is especially important to learn to notice how you react to the experience of solitude, whether you welcome it or typically avoid it.

I will be giving you practical techniques for seeing bad habits in action, and then gently encouraging new habits which will set you free to begin a deeper involvement with yourself.

For many of you, the reading of this book will coincide with a time in your life when you are in fact quite alone. Perhaps you think that what you need most is another person in your life, to make you happy again. Because we are social beings, there is of course a need for other people, but fundamentally the person you most need in your life is yourself. You will never be able to relate any more deeply with someone else than you are able to relate with yourself. It is equally true that if you don't really know yourself, you can never deeply know another person. A genuine friendship with yourself is the necessary model from which you form loving relationships with others. Without that foundation, we continue to act out the unsuccessful relationship patterns we have suffered from all our lives.

I know that the seemingly simple process of learning to relate more deeply and lovingly with yourself can be an extremely challenging one. You have to deal with many fears along the path to deeper self-love and understanding. But hopefully, you will gain adequate support and pragmatic guidance from our discussion in this book to move through apprehensions about facing and accepting who you really are.

Many people begin a process such as this with the firm conviction that they must change who they are; that they must transform their basic personalities if they are ever to resolve their problems and become the person they wish to be. But the reality of human personalities is that we cannot change who we are. We are stuck with ourselves, whether we like ourselves or not. We can grow and mature, and thereby expand and nurture our potential, but we will still always be ourselves. We cannot change our past. We need to learn to work within the basic personality structure we have inherited and developed, and to make the best of it—fundamentally to *accept* who we are.

In my professional career, I have never worked with anyone whose self-esteem became lower in the process of getting to know himself or herself better. Self-knowledge is an amazing healer. It carries within it a natural element of love and acceptance. People who do not accept themselves, people who claim they do not like themselves, people who say they are bored in their own presence, are simply people who do not know themselves very well. And to the extent that they are able to open up to get to know themselves better, they invariably begin to become interested in themselves more, to accept the inevitable flaws (give up the idea of having to be perfect!), and care for themselves more, as well.

Solitude is a powerful teacher. It is also a state in which we can find a great deal of pleasure and contentment in life. Silence, which is a major dimension of solitude, is also one of the essential qualities of a satisfied mind. In all the deep religious traditions of the world, solitude is seen as an essential ingredient in spiritual progress. But what is solitude on the inner level, and how can we enter into this prized state of mind?

The meditative techniques I will share with you are designed to open up a direct encounter with your deeper spiritual presence, without in any way coloring the experience with religious overtones that may be at odds with your own belief system, whatever it may be.

Once you make contact with the expansive, infinite center of your being, with the true you, so to speak, you will find that in fact, fundamentally, you are never alone. Your superficial sense of being alone will give way, as you continue the practice of looking inward, to a sense of participation in the vast interconnectedness of all existence. The spiritual metaphors of the ancient sages and the contemporary descriptions of interconnectedness of the new quantum physics both teach that there is no actual separateness possible in the universe. To say that all is one is a scientific as well as a spiritual statement. One of the most powerful ways to learn to live with yourself is to learn how to expand our consciousness in this way; by experiencing interconnectedness we develop a new experience of who we are.

In certain dimensions of consciousness, you are clearly a separate individual, all alone in life. At the same time, you are an integral part of the whole of life on this planet. To tap into this expanded sense of your involvement in life transforms your experience of solitude.

If we are in fact living in a universe that is intimately unified, then how is it possible for so many of us to go through life feeling terribly alone and isolated? In fact, it is our emotional and cognitive programming as children that leads us into our adult sense of isolation. In this book, we will explore specific techniques to confront this programming and move beyond the old emotions and attitudes that have led to feelings of isolation.

When I was about twenty, I first began to reflect on my own sense of isolation in life. Reading the New Testament one evening, I came to the passage where Jesus says to love your neighbor as you love yourself. I thought that was a foolish statement. I felt very little love for myself, which meant that I didn't have to love my neighbor very much either. But the essential message in that statement is that we must first expand our sense of self-love, if we are ever to truly love our neighbors. Jesus understood that the basis of love must begin with the fundamental acceptance of self.

Personal growth is not a matter of forming bigger and better concepts in the thinking part of our minds. Intellectual understanding of the need for self-love and regular periods of solitary reflection will help motivate us to begin the process. The real work, however, is in the experiential encounters with the inner realities that lie behind the concepts in our heads.

I will frequently be giving you time to put the book aside so you can actually try out techniques for exploring your consciousness, and it is important to take time with each of them and practice them regularly if you truly seek to grow in your relationship with yourself.

You will need to set aside at least a short period every day for reflection, meditation, and action in nurturing your relationship with your own inner spirit. You will need to create small bubbles of solitude in your life, to give yourself the regular opportunity to encounter yourself directly, alone, honestly, and with a heart more and more open to your own mysterious presence in the world right now.

Luckily, this way of exploring solitude is an enjoyable process. You will certainly encounter times when your old programming tends to turn the experience negative. At these times, you need to have patience with yourself and realize that each experience is a part of the process. If you follow the steps offered in this book, you should have little difficulty in tapping into the joy of living more intimately with yourself.

As a beginning, see what experience comes effortlessly to you right now, if you put the book aside and take a few deep breaths. Reflect patiently, kindly, on your present relationship with yourself. Do you like living with yourself?… Do you have a yes and no feeling about it?… What part of it is yes?… What part of it is no?…

CHAPTER ONE

Learning to Encounter Your Solitary Self

We often think of solitude as something that we may experience in our old age, but not during our younger years. In fact, solitude is a normal part of our lives, beginning in our earliest years. I was just outside peeking around the corner into my backyard, where my one-year-old is playing quite alone with himself and having a contented solitary experience, as he does for ten or fifteen minutes at a time, half a dozen times a day. He knows what it feels like to be alone already, and as long as he also gets enough loving attention and social interaction each day, he is quite eager to spend regular time alone with himself.

Each of us encountered solitude early in our lives. At times, we played alone and were quite content to do so, as long as we felt well-loved and protected. We knew how it felt to look around us and see no other human being. We experienced that primal sense of being alone in our bubble of perception.

The magic of solitude, of course, is that when there are no other human beings to relate with at the moment, our full attention can suddenly become focused on our own presence. We can be aware of all our sensory experiences, both internal and external. If we have learned to distrust solitude—perhaps to associate it with abandonment—this experience will be disturbing, or even frightening. If we have grown to love solitude, however, we may move quite naturally into the state of awareness where we realize directly the fact of being alive in the present moment.

When we suddenly experience ourselves fully present and participating in the life of the planet, we may have the sensation of being in harmony with our environs; of having an infinite inner universe inside us connected with an infinite outer universe around us. This ultimate experience comes to us most often when we pause alone and tune into the realm of solitude.

But of course almost all of us, while we were growing up, had quite different feelings when alone. At times, we felt lonely or afraid instead of contentedly alone. Instead of expanding awareness into a mystical feeling of unity with the world, we contracted into anxiety and loneliness, which instantly shatter the positive spirit of solitude.

Then, in an attempt to escape from the seemingly overwhelming power of solitude, we retreated from the intensity of the present moment and used our thinking mind to overcome the feeling of being alone. We imagined being with someone, for instance, or remembered being with someone, or made plans to go into action to find someone to be with, so that we could escape from pain. Or we distracted ourselves from the experience of solitude in other ways.

When deep down we don't feel adequately loved, we are more apt to react to solitude with the negative feeling of loneliness. Unfortunately, such habitual reactions against being alone serve to perpetuate a lonely existence. A negative attitude toward spending time alone makes us habitually deny ourselves the experience of solitude we actually require in order to break free of our lonely condition.

In this first chapter, I want to begin the process of guiding you into a more positive relationship with solitary moments in your everyday life. The first step in exploring your own feelings about solitude is to allow yourself to experience your own solitary presence.

Many of us are in the habit of instantly filling moments of solitude with mental busyness, using our thinking mind to avoid our own presence through sophisticated cognitive tricks that we have developed over the years. Usually, we do this without being aware of our strategies to avoid the experience of inner aloneness. Throughout this book, we will be learning basic techniques for breaking free of such limiting habits, so that when moments of solitude appear in each new day, we can take full advantage of them, to nurture our relationship with our own presence.

When living alone, it is easy to remain plugged into social inputs which keep us from having to encounter our solitary self. It is easy to distract ourselves by thinking about times in the past when we were involved in social interaction, or to fantasize about future encounters, or use the media to stimulate feelings of vicarious social encounter.

Because we are mostly unaware of these avoidance patterns, it is important to become conscious, more aware of how in fact we spend our time alone. In beginning to explore your self-relationship, the first thing to do is to take an honest look at how you habitually react to being alone. To what extent do you avoid regular encounters with your own inner self? How often do you pause and simply tune into your own presence in the present moment?

After you read this paragraph, I suggest that you put down the book and pause for a few moments to begin to explore how you react to being alone with yourself. Take a comfortable breath to release any tension, and notice your feelings as you sit alone… physical feelings, the sense of yourself in your body… and emotionally, what it actually feels like to be alone. Are you uneasy, restless, anxious? Do you immediately start thinking of other things you should be doing? Or fill your mind with all kinds of distractions?… Or can you stay relaxed with what's happening?… Observe your level of comfort or discomfort…

The next step is to look for positive experiences of solitude, to look back into your past, to remember times when you were alone and enjoyed being alone. Lonely people often believe they have never enjoyed being alone. But in almost every instance, this is not true; our memory can become so obsessed with painful experiences that it is easy to forget or deny the pleasurable experiences that did in fact occur.

So let me offer you a professional technique for opening up your memory banks, so that you can get beyond prevailing attitudes about solitude and tap into positive experiences of being alone. By allowing positive memories to become part of your conscious experience of solitude, you will make the first important step in creating a new, expansive concept of this vital element of your everyday life.

First of all, let's consider your present habits regarding solitude. How often yesterday, for instance, were you at least momentarily alone with yourself? And which, if any, of those solitary moments did you in fact enjoy?

The basic technique I want to teach you for accessing your memory banks is this: after reading the paragraph which presents you with a memory suggestion, put the book aside, close your eyes if this feels comfortable to you, and tune into your breathing. Think of memory not as "going back," but as "bringing forward" past experiences into the present moment. What you will be doing in remembering is to relive the sensory, emotional, and cognitive experiences you had at a certain moment in the past. And this process of reliving an experience is very much a present-moment experience.

Therefore, you will always need to first bring yourself fully into the present sensory moment, as preparation for a memory expedition. To do this, simply feel the air coming and going through your nose or mouth as you breathe. This instantly awakens your present-moment awareness. Then expand your awareness to include the sensations of movement in your chest and belly as you continue breathing. Then expand your awareness further to include perhaps your heartbeat or pulse, somewhere in your body. Then expand your awareness a final notch to include your entire body, here in the present moment. This simple meditation on present sensory experiences will prepare you to experience replays of perceptions and emotions from your past.

In order to awaken memories, you will want to choose a specific theme, such as any of those I suggest, and effortlessly let this suggestion run through your mind several times until memories start to be awakened in your mind and body. Continue being aware of your breathing, to stay conscious of the present moment, while the memories come. Awareness of your breathing helps you stay connected with experiences coming to you in the present-past continuum instead of losing yourself in a reverie of your past, and going relatively unconscious.

Take a few moments now to explore this meditation.

You can begin with a concrete suggestion to remember any periods of solitude you experienced yesterday or within the past week. After reading these meditation instructions, put the book aside and tune into the sensations you feel in your nose as you breathe... expand your awareness effortlessly to include the sensations of movement in your chest and belly as you breathe... expand your awareness to also include your heartbeat or pulse, somewhere in your body... and expand your awareness to include your whole body at once, here in the present moment... and while you remain aware of your breathing and body, say to yourself several times, "I want to remember times recently when I was alone, and enjoyed being alone"... and now just breathe into whatever memories come to you...

When I just went on this memory expedition to remember positive moments of solitude, I remembered first of all waking up and walking out onto my balcony from the bedroom, and looking out over the neighborhood. I stood there only a minute or two, but the experience was a beautiful one as I felt my waking consciousness rising to the surface of a new day. An early-morning aloneness break is a very important one to pause and experience fully. Many of us get up and rush into our daily routines without stopping to tune into our own presence. As a result, we miss an opportunity for self-awareness that can ground us and set a positive tone for the day.

In the morning, we also have solitary time in the bathroom; a meditative opportunity if we open ourselves to the aloneness experience that comes to us as we look ourselves face to face in the mirror and encounter our visual presence in the world. Again, tuning into one's breathing is the key for awakening the muse of solitude and self-awareness.

For those of us who commute to work, there are also many chances for solitary encounters with our own presence, if we take advantage of them. And at work there may be many short openings into the magic of solitude if we learn to tune into them whenever they occur.

Living near the ocean, yesterday I took time off from work and jumped in the car with my wife and baby, and headed for the beach. There were only about twenty people on the entire beach, so it was easy to choose social interaction or solitude, and I would guess that most of the people on the beach were there in search of some special hours of solitude; of communing with nature instead of being surrounded by man-made sights and sounds.

After an hour or so of great pleasure building sand castles with my little boy and playful wife, I felt that special urge come over me—that desire to retreat, to gain some distance from others—and I walked down the beach all alone. That urge is one we all know, even though we may then turn around and block the actual experience of solitude.

I thought of this as I walked down the beach, and was thankful that my wife and I have an understanding about the need for solitude. She also cherishes moments, even hours, of solitude, and from the beginning of our relationship, we talked of our personal needs, not only for intimacy but for the freedom to be alone.

What about your present relationships? Are you free to walk away, to ask for distance and space on a regular basis, or do the people you are close to feel you are rejecting them when you ask to be alone sometimes?

Take a few moments to look a little further into what you experienced recently when you were alone. After reading this paragraph, put the book aside, breathe… tune into your heartbeat… your whole body… enjoy being here in the present moment… and expand your experience to include recent memories, when you were with someone… did you feel free to ask for solitary space?… did you take time to be alone?…

were your needs for retreat and reflection respected by others?...

Looking further back into your past, you can begin a meditation process to allow memories of beautiful solitary times to come into your mind. This meditation for reliving moments of special solitary awareness is not a one-time exercise, but a rewarding and beneficial daily habit to adopt for the rest of your life. Now take a few minutes to do this "solitude remembrance" meditation, following the same technique you used in the previous exercise.

Begin by relaxing and tuning into your breathing... your heartbeat or pulse... your whole body here in the present moment... and expand your awareness to include memories of moments when you were alone, enjoying your own companionship, feeling your inner presence and the presence of the world around you, intimately... Notice the different memories that offer themselves... of special times... special places... quiet moments you may not have thought of in a long, long time... there may be memories that return over and over as you repeat this process...

Go through this simple reflective process at least once each day in the coming weeks if you want to tap into a very wonderful, powerful process for transforming your relationship with solitude. You will notice, even after just a few days, that your thoughts and attitudes about being alone will begin to change for the better. Through realizing the wonderful times you have had while alone with yourself, you will begin to experience a more positive emotional upsurge when you find yourself alone in the present moment.

As I sat on the beach yesterday and looked in the distance at the twenty solitary human beings on the beach with me, I was struck again by the remarkable fact that each and every one of us goes through our entire life completely within our own unique bubble of consciousness. We are unable to leave our bubble and trade bubbles with anyone else. All we can do is get to know our own bubble intimately, and learn how to expand our bubble of consciousness in satisfying ways.

When there is someone else with us, a strange thing usually happens to our bubble. We must contract it quite a bit, in order to hold our own internal center. Otherwise, the presence of the other person may overwhelm us and we may experience a severe contraction of our own consciousness. Often, we make this adjustment quite unconsciously, but if we are intensely engaged within our solitary space, this contraction will be more noticeable to us. See for yourself next time you move from solitary space to social space. Do you sense a constriction of your bubble of consciousness? Notice how different people affect your sense of that bubble. Also learn to notice exactly what you are experiencing, especially how it feels in your body to adapt to the presence of other people.

When you move in the other direction, from a social space to being alone, notice what happens to your consciousness. You are suddenly provided with the space to expand your consciousness infinitely in all directions! But what are your habits? Do you let go and relax into the bliss of solitary communion with the world around you, or do you contract against the fear of feeling lonely when alone?

Let me end this chapter by encouraging you to return to the "solitude-remembrance" meditation you did a few moments ago. This time, as you open yourself to reliving past experiences, think of a shift that you have made many times every day of your life. At one moment you are with one other person or in a group. The next moment you are alone, for a short time or a longer time… Discover for yourself what you feel, how you react, how your consciousness shifts when all at once you are in the intimate space of solitude… Discover for yourself what you do when moving from a social/intimate situation into a solitary situation…

CHAPTER TWO

Exploring and Healing Loneliness

It has often been said that loneliness has caused more suffering in the world than any other condition of the human spirit, and I would generally agree with the notion. When it is extreme, loneliness can plague a person's spirit, moment to moment, for an entire lifetime. It is also a feeling that almost everyone on the planet suffers from, at least now and then.

Loneliness does not come simply from being alone. In order to transcend loneliness, we first need to understand the source of this emotion and how it manifests as suffering in our bodies. Then we can explore ways of breaking free of its grip.

Loneliness is a condition that must be assessed honestly and clearly, and then dealt with through both action and reflection. You cannot just read a book and free yourself from loneliness by taking intellectual concepts and understandings, useful though they may be. Loneliness is actually an ingrained personality habit. It can be transcended in a two-part process. First, the memories, experiences, and beliefs that maintain loneliness in your consciousness must be understood and gently worked through. Second, the habit of loneliness must be replaced with more constructive, self-fulfilling emotional patterns.

If you experience extreme chronic loneliness, you may need more than written and auditory guidance such as this program provides. If you work to overcome chronic loneliness on your own, with the aid of this program, and are still unable to change your situation, you will do yourself a great favor by finding a professional to consult with in dealing with your condition.

This program provides a process of learning to live positively with oneself. Most people find the program adequate to free them from chronic loneliness, provided they commit themselves to exploring the actual experiences I will be guiding you through. Self-reflection and personal growth are not a magic experience, provided only in the confines of therapy. Once we learn professional techniques for achieving such growth, we are quite capable of helping ourselves move beyond old mental and emotional habits.

And let me say that feeling lonely now and then is not any kind of abnormal problem. Life is sometimes a lonely experience. We cannot entirely avoid this feeling as we progress through the years, and when balanced by periods of deep fulfillment on both inner and outer levels of relating, loneliness provides the impetus for growth that otherwise would not occur.

Loneliness becomes a problem only when it sets up housekeeping in the middle of our lives and refuses to go away. I suspect almost all of us have had at least one prolonged bout of loneliness that lasted weeks, months, even years. I went through almost two years of feeling very lonely most of the time, after the collapse of my first marriage. It was hell—but it was also the time during which I had my deepest insights into not only the nature of human living in general, but also into the particular programmed foibles that were reflected in my personal life.

We are curious beings, in that we tend to do most of our growing only when provoked by pain, discomfort, or crisis of one kind or another. As long as everything is going well, most of us are inclined to relax and cruise through the days without pushing ourselves to mature and expand our sense of who we are and what we might do in life. But in life, we regularly encounter situations that do cause us pain and suffering, that do challenge our present way of living our lives.

The feeling of loneliness, like any other pain we

might experience, functions as an indicator that something is wrong in our lives. When taken as a signal, a symptom trying to get our attention so that we can deal with an underlying problem, loneliness is perhaps our very best friend. Loneliness stimulates us to develop good relationships with others and ourselves, to create experiences that can prove ultimately rewarding in our lives.

So perhaps the beginning point in dealing with loneliness should be thankfulness that the emotional pain of loneliness does exist inside us. It pushes us out into the world to satisfy our interpersonal needs. Otherwise, we might retreat entirely into our solitary worlds and sever our connection with others. And as I mentioned earlier, it is the balance of solitude and socializing that makes for a full experience as a human being.

In dealing with loneliness, we must first recognize how it originates in the human body and spirit. We are creatures with instinctual reactions and emotions, and we are all born with a genetically programmed reaction called the fear of abandonment. Babies have this fear, with the emotional reaction of crying when they feel they might have been forgotten and left behind. Abandonment is experienced by babies as the most fundamental threat to their survival. This inherited reaction obviously had great survival value when we were living in primitive nomadic conditions, hundreds of thousands of years ago.

But we still carry this primal fear of abandonment with us. Babies still need to express their need for care and attention, and adults need to be reminded how their children are feeling. As little children, we may have felt the fear of abandonment very often when our parents left us alone or with strangers at a sensitive age, and disappeared from our present-moment world. Later, we may have felt neglected or rejected by other relatives or by friends. We reacted automatically with the emotion that we would develop into a pattern of loneliness.

So loneliness has its origins deep within our genetic makeup. It is not a learned reaction, at least in the beginning. And because the fear of abandonment is so primal and runs so deep in our human make-up, the feeling of loneliness can take us way beyond our rational minds and overwhelm us with its power.

As human beings we are also thinking creatures. As we grow up, we learn to use our minds to repeat experiences from our past, to dwell on memories rather than remaining completely in the present moment as most other creatures on this planet do. And by remembering traumatic experiences that induced the feelings of abandonment and loneliness, we can in fact chronically restimulate these feelings, even though the actual situation that produced them has long since passed from our lives.

Here we find the source of most of our lonely feelings as adults. We often feel as emotionally shattered as a child when we experience abandonment, because the present-moment experience takes us back to something we experienced when we were very young. The roots of a present-moment abandonment lie deep in childhood; the present situation is a replay of the earlier one.

We can recover from this loneliness as we work through the grief and fear brought on by the original experience, whether it was a temporary separation or the loss of someone we loved. Once this is done, feelings about our present situation can be more easily overcome, or they may disappear, because we have healed something within ourselves.

Chronic lonely feelings are in fact generated by memory, not just by the emotional center of the brain. People who feel habitually lonely are in fact caught up in repeating mental flows that provoke the emotional response of loneliness. And the way to break free of such a condition is to deal with your cognitive habits, not just your emotional reactions to the cognitive habits.

If you chronically feel lonely, certain beliefs, thoughts, attitudes, and buried memories must be running through your mind, day in and day out, stimulating this chronic emotional state. The challenge is to begin to realize what in fact your mind is habitually doing.

In this regard, your mind is quite similar to a computer that is programmed to do the same thing over and over again. All mental programming elicits repetitive behavior and emotional reactions—that is part of our equipment for maintaining stability in our lives. In order to break free of undesirable programming, you must access the computer, look at the problem, and introduce a new program that creates more satisfying patterns in your life.

As you know, however, old habits can be quite difficult to break. In fact, we have found that mental programming cannot be erased from the human mind, short of damaging the brain itself. An important element in transcending negative mental programming is to introduce new programming, a new habit, a new behavioral and cognitive pattern that is more rewarding. When this happens, the old programming simply stops receiving energy to function, and falls dormant.

It must be understood that personal growth is not achieved by attacking our old programming. It simply asks us to shift our attention and energy away from the old programming and in the direction of a more satisfying, consciously chosen, new habit. New cognitive programming will begin to replace the old habit based on the pleasure principle: the new pattern brings a more positive, pleasurable dimension to our lives.

In working with loneliness, you will first need to develop a regular habit of observing how your mind keeps creating that emotional state. This habit is something you can develop by pausing at various times of the day to observe yourself.

I'd like you to take a few minutes to imagine yourself going through your ordinary day... beginning in the morning. Pause to notice what thoughts and attitudes typically run through your mind as you go out in the world... as you come in contact with other people... as you do your work... note what thoughts and attitudes echo or reinforce feelings of loneliness... What are the almost subliminal memories and attitudes that color your experience with lonely feelings?...

As you develop this habit of self-observation, you will begin to see how you sustain negative patterns of various kinds in your consciousness. This will help you to more clearly identify early memories and beliefs from which chronic or habitual feelings of loneliness may have developed.

As children, we naturally identified our own sense of being with that of our parents, or with at least one person who nurtured us through childhood. Then in adulthood, we found other people to take the place of our parents in most cases, and formed new intimate relationships, to give us that primal feeling of being cared for by someone we identified with.

When such relationships break up, we are likely to suffer a terrible feeling of abandonment, and loneliness results until we either finally find our own separate sense of identity in full maturity, or we find someone else to latch onto as a new parental figure in our lives.

What I challenge you to do as you read and reflect on the exercises in this book is to look back on specific incidents or circumstances in your childhood, and then in your adult life, where you have felt abandoned, and reacted with severe loneliness. By honestly seeing the origins of loneliness in your present life, you will make the first step toward transcending your lonely feelings.

In therapy, I have found that most people are not very clear about the origins of their abandonment complexes. They tend to naturally fixate on the most recent feeling of loss, usually a broken sexual relationship, and think that this one experience is the entire source of their loneliness. But in fact, this most recent loss is only the last in a series of similar experiences. And to resolve abandonment feelings once and for all, it is essential to first look at all the losses and experiences of separation, move through the feelings of grief and anger, and accept this history for what it is.

Life is a constant progression from total union with our mothers in the womb, to separation at birth, then further separation during infancy and childhood as we develop our own lives, and finally physical separation as we move into adulthood and leave our parents behind so that we can form new intimate bonds and create a life of our own. The human personality normally develops, step by step, to match this separation from the parents. Hopefully, the child's inner sense of worth and identity grows in step with the external requirements of separation from parents, so that there is little trauma.

But every new distancing from the parents is a point in our history when we can feel abandoned. And when we are not ready to take a new step out on our own, the result is an experience of abandonment and a programming of loneliness. Already, there have been times when my wife and I have felt it necessary to push our little boy a bit into his own confrontation with himself, so that he realizes that sometimes we are not constantly there for him right when he demands our attention. We see him act hurt and angry, and our parenting instincts hopefully guide us in our progressive separating of ourselves from the center of his own inner universe. The job of parenting does include this difficult challenge of encouraging the development of independent identity in a child. The challenge, of course, is to give that encouragement at the right time, in the right amount.

Parenting is a job that no one has ever done perfectly. All children have suffered from feelings of abandonment and have at times felt lonely; we parents have not always perfectly timed with their stimulation of the separation process and the development of individuality. Growing up is, in part, a struggle with our own developing emotions as we learn to face life a little more on our own. It is also true that some children are given too little stimulation and must struggle to free themselves from parental domination.

Many children in our culture face the situation of premature separation, especially in families split by divorce or affected by parents' spending too little time with them. Other children experience separation because the parents, although physically present, do not provide enough love and nurturing because of their own early experiences of deprivation. Although the intention of the parents is not usually to abandon their children, the children experience premature separation—whatever the cause—as abandonment.

As adults, our challenge is to look back and realize what happened to us as we were growing up. We must accept the parenting job our parents did with us for what it was, see how it programmed our minds and emotions, and then act on our own to heal old emotional wounds and develop more mature emotional patterns.

In the previous chapter, you explored the actual moment-to-moment experience of solitude, how you react to it, and how you experience moving between solitary and social space. You have also looked at how you maintain negative emotional patterns through memories, habitual thought patterns, and attitudes. Since it is clear that these current experiences are all shaped and colored by earlier experiences in life—by memories, both positive and negative—the next step is to begin to explore the memories that are the source of those emotional patterns.

The challenge is to relive your history of separation, loneliness, and abandonment without again becoming lost in the pain and simply repeating it. Repeating the suffering is actually an abandonment of yourself. That is another reason I stress that you remain in the present as you do these meditative memory exercises, always staying in contact with your breath, aware of yourself physically in the present moment. In this way, you learn to be with yourself, to give yourself the support you needed but didn't get during past moments of trauma. You become your witness and your support. As you do this, you will find that little by little your relationship to the memories changes and you begin to heal. We have all experienced abandonment; what we need to learn is to never abandon our own self.

After reading this paragraph, put the book aside and tune into your breathing without any effort... tune into your heartbeat or pulse... allow yourself the time to feel your whole body here in the present moment... Begin to look back to times when you experienced a painful sense of loss, abandonment, or loneliness when you were very young... and remember that you, the adult, are now here to support that child... Keep on breathing calmly as the memories come up…

When we find ourselves alone, we may tend to feel solitude as an emptiness. But there is the possibility of learning to relate to this emptiness in a positive way, so that the emptiness is not empty but filled with our own solitary presence.

Your breathing is the model. Every exhale is an emptying experience. The air you just took into your innermost center, the air you have merged with in your lungs and bloodstream, gets pushed out and is lost to you. At the bottom of your exhale, you experience emptiness: imagine it as a moment with your solitary presence… Then comes the natural inhale, once again the filling up, the new encounter with the outside world inside you…then the urge to exhale that air, to be empty again in your solitary presence… Consciously nurture your relationship with emptiness. As you cultivate your appreciation for this "emptiness," loneliness will, step by step, become a thing of the past.

CHAPTER THREE

Becoming Your Own Best Friend

Part I: First Steps

As you sit here reading these words, it might be helpful to consider who your real friends are right now. Who really cares for you the most these days? Who can you turn to for support and love, who can you trust to be there when you need encouragement and acceptance?

The curious thing about a friend is that this person, no matter how much he or she loves you, still considers himself or herself more important than you. Ultimately, each of us must first pledge allegiance to our own selves. Then, with what energies and love we have left over, we can reach out and offer support to a few people we care very much for. As I mentioned, Jesus presented us with the challenge of loving our neighbor as much as we love ourselves, but not more. Within the Christian tradition, however, the notion developed that human beings should act in selfless ways, denying their own needs in order to help others. In fact, to be selfish has always been considered somewhat sinful. To view yourself as the most important person in your life may be judged un-Christian.

Many clients I have worked with were seriously hampered in their ability to love and be best friends with themselves, specifically because, as children, they were strongly programmed with this notion of interacting with the outside world, selflessly. Whenever they felt a natural desire to put themselves first in life, to be their own best friend, they felt pangs of guilt for their supposed transgression of their Christian faith. As they grew up, they constantly battled against their desire to take time to nurture their own personalities and to find ways to satisfy their own needs.

During my early twenties, I worked as a minister in a Christian church. I observed, first-hand, the conflicts that many Christians experience around the idea of focusing loving attention on their own inner needs. In fact, I have been attacked many times by Christian teachers and writers who object to my insistence that we must first improve our own consciousness and habits if we are ever to be of help to others around us.

Of course it is true that many people do overindulge the pleasures of their own little bubble of reality, to the exclusion of ever turning to help others. But it is also true that a great deal of the supposed help that people offer backfires and ultimately interferes with the natural development of those they are trying to help.

It seems helpful to turn to Jesus's words that say we should love and help those around us in the same way that we love and help ourselves. This motto provides a healthy balance, a clear guideline.

One of my purposes in writing this book is certainly to help you move into a more fruitful position from which to offer your love and help to other people. In quite simple terms, as you learn to be a better friend to yourself, you will almost automatically start being a better friend to others. This equation is borne out by tried and true observation—the more love you feel for yourself, the more love you will have to share with others. Love is a marvelous thing, in that there is a seemingly infinite amount of the mysterious stuff in the universe. Our challenge is to learn how to bring it into our own being and then let it spread freely to those around us.

In the beginning of this chapter, I asked you who your best friend is these days. If you answered anyone but yourself, this may say something about your relationship with yourself. At least it may indicate that you have not thought much about it as an actual relationship. It *is* a relationship, the most fundamental one in your life.

Take a few moments to pause now and think about that relationship. First, tune into your breathing… your heartbeat… the sense of your physical presence… and reflect on this relationship… on the idea of becoming your own best friend… how you feel about that… and what it would mean in practical terms in your life… As your own best friend, what would you do that is different from what you do now?…

There is a very good reason for each of us to become our own best friend. No one else can know, as well as we can, what we need in life, and how we can best go about getting what we need to live a worthwhile, fulfilling life. It makes perfect sense for each of us to first take responsibility for getting our own lives in shape.

Let's look a bit deeper into the dynamics involved in being our own best friend. First of all, a "relationship" requires an "other" to relate to. Who is available to relate to whom within our internal universe? If you are to be your own best friend, in a sense there must be at least two complementary or opposite presences to relate with each other. If we are to be our own best friend, there must be a sense of polarity in our internal system.

There are in fact a multitude of different presences within each and every one of us. At the most basic levels, for instance, there is our thinking, cognitive mind, in contrast to our physical, feeling body. And because our thinking mind is usually running our personal show, the question arises: to what extent is our thinking mind a good loving friend to our physical body? Are we concerned about the physical health of our body? Do we get enough exercise, eat good food, sleep well, and satisfy our body's basic emotional needs, or are we the kind of friend who doesn't really stay in touch with our body enough to make sure that the physical part of us is healthy and happy?

To be best friends with your body is a magnificent challenge. And to be a negligent friend of your body is one of the most dangerous and terrible things you can do to yourself. You, as a thinking, observant person, are fully responsible for the remarkable living entity that is your body. And your stewardship of the physical presence you have been given is your most basic loving task in life. To what extent have you fully realized this stewardship, and to what extent are you successful in taking maximum care of your body?

Take a few moments to put the book aside and tune into your breath... tune into your physical body, each part of it, and your body as a whole... consider if you are best friends with your body... and how you show your caring... or your lack of it...

The trick to mind/body friendship is simple, but often overlooked. The human body is an organism that functions basically on pain/pleasure programming. The human body desires pleasure and abhors pain. By pleasure, I do not mean just sensory stimulation of a positive kind, although that dimension of pleasure is very important. By pleasure, I mean the feeling of vitality, of health, of purpose, of engagement and connection to the present moment of life.

I'm sure you have known many moments when you felt on top of the world, when your body felt full of positive energy and contentment. When you love someone else, this is how you want them to feel in their body, right? So if you love yourself, you will want to optimize your body's opportunity to feel this way, too.

Let me give you some potent sentences to play with, to stimulate insight into your relationship with your body. These statements are often used in therapy to awaken a new level of interaction between a person's thinking mind and feeling body. Some of the statements are of a positive nature; some of them are negative. They will provoke you either to agree or disagree, or they will provoke mixed reactions. You may find that on some levels of consciousness, you agree, while on other levels you might discover that you disagree with what a statement expresses. And as you move through the reflections and meditations in this book, your under-standing of yourself will increase and your reactions to the statements will change, as well.

So take these sentences as catalysts to stimulate a deeper realization of your present relationship with your body. Over the next few weeks, regularly open the book to this page and say some of these sentences to yourself, and then breathe into whatever responses or reactions arise from deep within you. Try saying them aloud, to see how much more provocative this can make the experience.

Begin by reading the sentence... then say it to yourself... say it aloud if you wish... then close your eyes... breathe... and open yourself to whatever thoughts and feelings rise to the surface as you let the statement pass through you and resonate in your mind and body:

1) I want my body to feel good.
2) I feel ashamed when I have the desire to do something that would make my body feel really good.
3) I don't really like my body. It's not good enough.
4) Sometimes I'm sorry for how I treat my body.
5) I'm afraid of what I might do in life if I fully surrendered to physical pleasure.
6) It somehow doesn't seem right to want to feel good in my body all the time.
7) I don't know how to love myself.
8) The human body is nothing more than a vehicle for the spirit to do its work through.
9) Ah, I really do love my body!
10) There isn't any difference, any separation between my mind and my body—they are one and the same presence.

Since the thinking mind arises from physical components of the body, we can state that there is in fact no separation between mind and body. They are a continuum that cannot in any way be broken or dissected. But our experience does create the sense of separation, and this inner experience is our guide to understanding the inner dynamics of the mind/body relationship. You certainly know what it is like to get lost in thought and to lose awareness of your body, literally for hours at a time. You do have the ability to forget your body completely, as if it were a separate thing and not part of you.

But at some point, your body manages to get your attention, usually through sending messages of pain or hunger into the center of your thinking consciousness, thus forcing you to take a break from your thinking or activity to attend to your physical needs.

In actuality, your brain contains regions that are devoted to your thinking mind and regions that are devoted to your physical well-being and enjoyment. The habits you establish in childhood of how these regions of your mind interact determine your relationship between your thinking mind and your body.

Since this interaction is mostly unconscious, it usually takes a certain amount of reflection and observation to become aware of your patterns of mind/body relating.

To begin with, take a few moments to consider the programming you received from your parents that influenced how you relate to your body. Consider your father as a model. Did he love his body, was he best friends with his body, or did he have the habit of denying his body, of abusing it, of being its enemy instead of its friend?... Pause for a few moments, close your eyes perhaps, tune into your breathing, and let memories come, of your father and his relationship with his own body... What messages did he give you about your own body?

And what about your mother? Was she in a harmonious, honest, loving relationship with her body, or did she have attitudes about her body that made her treat her body as less than her best friend?... What messages did she pass on to you about relating to your body?... Pause and go deeply into these questions...

Next consider the community you grew up in. What was the prevailing attitude toward the body in your community—among your friends and extended family and other adults you knew? Did you pick up positive loving attitudes toward your body from these people, or did they tend to abuse and disregard their bodies?...

And right now, what is your attitude toward your body?... Have you been in tune with your physical feelings and needs while reading these pages, or have you been mostly out of your body while reading about your relationship with your body?... Pause for a few moments, and tune into your body... Notice how you feel in your body right now... Notice how your emotions connect with that feeling... Do you like your body right now and the way it feels?... Or do you have some judgments about your body?... How important is it to you right now that your body feel good?... You expect your body to function in a way that you like, but are you patient and caring enough to satisfy its needs?...

In your relationship with yourself, there are countless different dimensions of your personality to explore. Internally, you are a community of presences that continually react with each other. There is the little boy or girl within you, for instance, in contrast to the mature man or woman. There is a teenager within you. There is a male part within each woman; a female part within each man. There is the wild, passionate lover within you, in contrast to the practical thinker and sober philosopher. There is the emotional part of you that is

completely caught up in feelings of love and anger, playfulness and despair, excitement and depression, joyful-
ness and anxiety. And in contrast to this emotional part
of you, there is the cold analytical part that seeks truth
and objective perception. There is the survivor in you,
and there is also the goof-off. There is the creator in you,
and also the destroyer. You are full of opposites. You are
full of the selves you were at different times in your life.
You are also full of all the different people you have
known in life. You have your mother inside you, and
your father; you have teachers inside you; you have
friends and lovers. You are full of different feelings and
personages and desires and attitudes. You are a vastness;
a constantly changing presence.

And very often, different aspects of your personality rise up at the same time and are present in your consciousness as either friends or combatants.

In most personalities, there is a dominant judgmental presence that believes that it ought to run the
show. It may be a harsh dictator to your spirit in its various dimensions, or a kind loving friend to all these
dimensions. It may have stern or mellow moods,
depending on how your life is going.

The key question, of course, is the dominant tendency of your judgmental presence and its relationship

with all the qualities, desires, personages, and tendencies you contain within you.

Let's look honestly at your ruling presence. Since your relationship with yourself is determined mainly by the judgmental function of your mind, it is important to explore the dominant attitudes and mental habits that determine what comes into your mind; what you think, what you let yourself feel and do in life. None of us is free of the domination of our prevailing attitudes and habits. And if we want to expand and grow—if we want to gain more freedom of expression and enjoyment of life—then we must look to our power center. This is the real challenge. Who is in charge? Deep down, are we satisfied with the programming that is running most of our inner life?

To gain insight into this programming, this reflexive mental functioning that judges and determines what dimensions of our personality are permitted to express themselves, we must learn the trick of stepping back a certain distance from the busyness of our thinking minds. We must learn to create a separation between our attention and the cognitive activities of our mind—in other words, learn to witness our mind in action.

This separation allows the inner friendship to develop because it creates space for reflection and for gaining perspective on ourselves. With this perspective, we can take a look at those judgments and open ourselves to the possibility of accepting our whole being. This open-hearted approach is the basic requirement for developing a fulfilling inner relationship.

I give all my clients a basic meditation practice that can be done sitting quietly alone or at any time as you go about your daily life. It is simply to observe the judgmental functioning of your mind:

To develop this habit of observation, start by becoming aware of your breath. This will let you observe your mind in action. Notice what impulses are judged as good, and as bad. Notice what thoughts are pushed aside in your mind, and which ones are encouraged... Notice how you value yourself—how you rate yourself, your abilities, your qualities... Notice if there is a heart connection between your mind and your body, or if your mind seems to run without feeling... And notice which dominant emotions your mind is chronically stimulating within you. As you go through your day, notice what tapes your mind runs over and over that trigger these feelings...

Be aware of your breathing first, and then let your awareness expand to observe your mind in action. By placing your primary awareness on your breathing, you then establish the needed distance from your thinking mind, so that there exists a sense of perspective. Only with perspective can we in fact observe. Let awareness of your breathing open your perspective. This exercise is very simple, and yet ultimately deep. I teach it in almost all my books because it is a basic tool for the expansion of consciousness that creates personality growth.

The distance you create from your thinking mind allows you to observe its patterns. Only when you regularly become aware of the content of judgments and other negative mental habits can you expect to change them. As you observe, breathe gently through the patterns; you will find that, little by little, you will give them less energy and let them go. The other benefit of this exercise is to help you become more aware of the fundamental self that exists beyond the busyness of the patterns of the thinking mind. If you want to live more fully with yourself, you need to develop this dual habit of self-observation: to note and breathe through the thinking patterns, and to become more and more conscious of your fundamental self.

To discover yourself, you need to develop the habit

of looking within. The simplest guidepost or reference point is your breathing. If you are aware of your breathing, you are looking within. Then you will begin to see more and more of yourself in action. And you will never see yourself except in action because there is no stopping of the show of consciousness. You cannot freeze-frame yourself. You can only see the show in action.

Notice that your breathing is always in action. Even when you hold your breath, in the middle of your breathing you will find your heart beating. The realities of breathing and heart-beating are deeper internal events than any thoughts that might be running through your mind. So by focusing on them, you gain a deeper perspective on fundamental self. Use the following meditation frequently to help you develop the habit of self-observation.

Take a few moments now to begin to explore that deeper perspective… Tune into your breathing… Tune into the sensation of the air rushing in through your nose, flowing out through your nose… At the same time, tune into the sensation of your heartbeat and pulse…Think first about becoming friends with your body. Focus attention on your body so that a relationship can expand and develop… When you have a sense of your body as a whole, let your attention flow a little deeper, toward the center of your own being... Imagine a friendship developing with all the various dimensions that exist like planets in orbit around your center...

Who are you? Who is there for your mind to relate with, to be best friends with? You alone are in position to relate with your deeper spirit, directly. But friendship requires attention. It requires regular contact. It requires acceptance of whatever you discover about yourself. It requires an opening of your heart to allow your various dimensions to feel loved, to feel free to express themselves through the vehicle of your actions and expressions.

Take a few moments to reflect. What would happen if you took time every day to nurture your own relationship with yourself?... How would it change your own life?... How would the rest of the world benefit if you were in a deeper loving relationship with yourself?... Let these questions reverberate within you as you practice your self-awareness meditation each day...

CHAPTER FOUR

Becoming Your Own Best Friend

Part II: Self-Acceptance

The deepest obstacle to learning to become one's best friend is the challenge of total self-acceptance. One of the main reasons we tend to spend so little time hanging out enjoyably with ourselves is that we simply do not accept many aspects of ourselves. Instead, we habitually condemn certain qualities that threaten our concept of who we should be.

If only we could make those bothersome and sometimes downright embarrassing parts of us go away permanently by ignoring them and pretending they don't exist, then perhaps the policy of not paying any attention to our own selves would work. But in fact we never get away from ourselves. And by trying to ignore parts of ourselves by not turning our attention inward, we unfortunately cause these parts to become more bothersome than they would be if we accepted them and worked with them toward our common cause of living a full and satisfying life.

We limit and define ourselves by rejecting parts of who we are. When we deny the vastness of our inner life, when we fail to accept and love who we naturally are, then two things happen: we virtually starve our own spirit, and we are experienced by others as shallow, remote, or lacking in warmth. Both situations interfere with our fundamental well-being and happiness.

In this chapter, I want to guide you through the same evaluation of your judgmental habits as I would if we were working together, and then show you some direct ways in which you can begin to improve your self-acceptance.

As we found in the previous chapter, your cognitive mind is responsible for judging your thoughts, feelings, and actions. So we will need to continue the basic task of exploring how you do judge yourself, and how you can break free of negative habits of judgment.

Discrimination is a function of the human mind that is not at all negative in itself. We do need to learn how to tell the difference between extremes in life, and to evaluate what seems good for us in our daily routines and what seems to be bothersome. Our personalities develop along these lines as experience teaches us what seems best to do in life, and what seems best to avoid.

Realistic self-evaluation is certainly of value, as

well. Even constructive criticism of our own thoughts, feelings, and actions is very helpful in developing an optimum way of going about life.

What is maladaptive is chronic negative self-judgment based on severe rules and regulations, ethics, and anxieties. While growing up, each of us began to develop a basic self-image that reflected both what we were taught about ourselves by feedback from outside, and what we experienced from the inside about ourselves. The sum total of our learning and experience resulted in a dominant attitude or set of attitudes about our self-worth, our natural abilities, our right to enjoy life, and our sense of duty.

When properly nurtured, children will quite naturally develop a self-image that is positive and that matches their talents and limitations. They will accept who they are and feel good about themselves unless they do something that violates their healthy image of who they are and what they should do in life.

But a terribly large percentage of children grow up in distorted, judgmental environments. They are taught that they are somehow sinful, degraded, or inferior by nature, and that no matter what they do, deep down they will remain ugly, worthless, or not good enough. At times there are religious overtones to these judgments, but usually parents themselves are the perpetrators of negative self-images in their children. When parents themselves feel low self-esteem, they will unconsciously pass on this negative attitudinal inheritance to their children. This goes on, generation after generation, unless the offspring consciously act to free themselves from judgmental programming.

The base line of judgment is of course this: are you okay, are you naturally acceptable in your own eyes? Or are you not okay—are you somehow below the mark, ugly, stupid, unacceptably confused, neurotic, weak, ignorant, degenerate? It doesn't matter what scale you are judging yourself upon. What matters is the final judgment of okay, or not okay.

Never have I had a client come into my therapy office who felt generally okay about himself or herself. Always, the dominant personality condition is a chronic self-judgment of not being okay, of not accepting oneself as is. The aim in therapy, or in working with a program such as this, is to improve self-image, engender a sense of self-love, and defuse the chronic judgmental function of the cognitive mind.

Take a few moments now to reflect on your self-image. How do you see yourself? Are you okay, or aren't you? Can you accept yourself just as you are, with all your problems and limitations, weaknesses and faults?... Or are you standing in judgment of yourself, condemning your natural spirit to living within an interior torture chamber?... Pause, breathe, let insights come...

Friendship implies acceptance and compassion. It might be said that true friendship is more an acceptance of imperfection than an admiration of perfection. And what is true in being friends with others is equally true in being friends with ourselves. Obviously, if we are going to enjoy being alone with ourselves, we are going to have to be friends with ourselves. And this means accepting our own imperfections, having compassion for our weaknesses, loving ourselves just as we are, not withholding love until we are what we want ourselves to become.

Some parents place such grand expectations on the shoulders of their children that the children have almost no room just to be themselves as they are in the present moment. Many parents chronically push their kids to attain higher and higher levels of accomplishment. In order to be loved, these children feel they must always strive to be more than they presently are.

The result is a personality structure that simply isn't patterend to gain satisfaction in the present moment. Everything is aimed at getting better and better, rather than accepting and enjoying things right now. The ideal image of the person is never the same as the actual image. Thus there is no chance of a relaxed sense of happiness in the present moment. The mind is always comparing and contrasting the present level of attainment with an ideal level of attainment. And as soon as a goal has been reached, the mind creates new levels of ideal attainment to strive for. This neurotic condition of the human spirit has become nearly universal in our highly competitive society.

We are taught to be afraid that if we accept ourselves just as we are, with all our imperfections and lack of ultimate attainment of our goals, we will lose our drive to advance in life. This is a monstrous fear, because it is not based on the reality of human evolution. The truth is that when we accept ourselves as we are in the present moment, we do continue to grow, to advance quite naturally. We don't need a judgmental pressure to push us, unless we want to push ourselves beyond our natural limits.

But our society stresses pushing beyond natural limits, and values future attainment over contentment and present-moment enjoyments. The result is a civilization of discontented people, not because we don't have very much, but because we don't know how to enjoy what we do have. We continue to play into the commercial dynamics of our culture, and thus to be victims of the economic system. We reach a point where we gain the riches of the world, but lose our inner freedom in the process.

We lose our sense of satisfaction with not only what we have, but with who we are. We lose the ability to pause, to settle into quiet moments with ourselves, and to enjoy the simple experience of just being. As soon as we pause for a moment, we are conditioned to feel uneasy, guilty for being lazy perhaps, or anxious that something bad will happen to us if we indulge in doing nothing for a while. And perhaps we feel guilty for retreating even from social interaction.

Since truly independent thought is incompatible with political control, governments do not encourage private citizens to take time off to reflect on life. Solitary reflection is not a social act; it cannot be tracked, recorded, brought into the mainstream of life in which political and economic power operate. When people are inwardly free and content, they are less susceptible to the subterfuges of power and the lure of consumerism.

In an age of media saturation and consumerism, learning to live contentedly with yourself is therefore something of a revolutionary act. When you learn how to retreat into solitary space regularly and be content with your own company, you are setting yourself free from much of the manipulation that surrounds you.

The joke is this—almost all of us are in fact quite okay just the way we are. We need to tune into who we really are beyond our superficial programming. We have bodies that are working fairly well, minds that are functioning fairly well. All we lack is the ability to enjoy what we have.

✗ What is wrong with you now, right now? Perhaps you have some health problem, or some financial problem, or some emotional problem. So what? Nobody's perfect. You can struggle to solve your existing problem, while at the same time accepting that the problem exists. You need to know that it is perfectly okay to have problems. This is not easy, because we tend not to feel okay about ourselves when we have problems. It is a great challenge to learn to accept yourself, like yourself, no matter what is happening in your life.

As children, our logic puts cause and effect together in naive ways. We tend to think, for example, that if bad things happen to us, we must ourselves be bad. We also, as children, have a naive belief in our own power that makes us think we are the cause of bad things that happen to other people. The programming that teaches us to feel that we are not okay just the way we are comes from many sources, but the primary source is other people: how they view us, how they view themselves, how they treat us, how parents have been taught to raise children. Less than two generations ago, parents were sternly advised by experts not to show love and affection for their children, for fear of spoiling them and making them unable to cope with the outside world. Babies were fed on rigid, doctor-prescribed schedules that took no account of their needs. As a society, we are still dealing with the fallout of past child-raising theories, repressive sexual attitudes, and guilt based on religious beliefs, as well as the psychological problems of individual families.

As individuals we need to do our best to sort out the different threads of our programming, not in order to blame but in order to understand what has warped our thinking and to free ourselves. In this process, we will eventually come to the need to forgive. To free ourselves fully from the programming of parents or others who may have taught us to judge ourselves harshly, we need to forgive those people and move on.

Take time now, and during the next few weeks and months, to explore how you were taught that you are not perfectly okay just as you are... Look back to your childhood, find out who and what programmmed you to judge yourself... Were there things that you blamed yourself for because of your childlike way of thinking?... As you understand what happened to you, notice whether you are ready to forgive anyone— including yourself—who harmed you by imposing negative judgments... and separate yourself from the negative programming... Remember that there are many ways that you may have taken in judgments about yourself... from feelings about you that you took in... from discipline or restrictions that were imposed on you... from feeling neglected, rejected, or abandoned by those you cared about... from your child logic that told you if you feel bad, you must *be* bad, not worth anything... and from actual judgmental words... Look back now for a few moments as you put the book aside... tune into your breathing, and see what memories come to mind...

Once we have begun to identify the sources of this

early negative self-judgment, the first step is to look at them from a mature perspective and recognize just how harmful these judgments are to our spirit. And we need to develop the habit of noticing the part they play in our life. Fundamentally, though, we can't reason them away. In trying to escape from negative self-judgments, we have a natural tendency to struggle against them directly. That is, we try to overcome our thinking mind with our thinking mind. We may find ourselves doing battle within the conceptual framework of judgment, attempting to alter our programming so that we judge ourselves positively instead of negatively.

While it is useful to recognize our intrinsic value and to understand the dynamics of inner judgment, we need to step outside the judgmental process altogether if we wish to change emotionally ingrained patterns. When it comes to self-worth, we need to shift our focus of attention away from the cognitive process of the mind and into an expanded sense of whole-body awareness. In this expanded awareness, which transcends the thinking mind, comes a direct experience of just being in the present moment. There is no judgment of acceptable or unacceptable.

Within the whole-body awareness, our focus needs to shift to the heart, both physically and spiritually.

When we become preoccupied with negative judgments, our mind becomes estranged from our heart
and from our physical self as a whole. To be satisfied
and contented, we need to bring mind and heart
together again. It is by disassociating mind from heart
that dissatisfaction comes about. People who are cen-
tered in their hearts are almost always good friends with
themselves. Even if they are financially poor, they have a
vast wealth of heart satisfaction to balance their poverty.
But to be the other way around—with great gobs of
money and no contact with one's heart—this is the true
poverty.

So let me give you a heart meditation that you can
bring into your moments of solitude, to begin to free
yourself of your self-inflicted prison of the mind. The
trick is to realize that you have the ready ability to
choose where to focus your attention: on thinking, or
on the feelings that reside in your heart. By shifting your
attention to your heart region as a conscious decision,
you in fact bring yourself into contact with the part of
you that gives you the feeling of not being alone. You
liberate yourself from the unfeeling emptiness of stale
ideas and concepts, and break free into the fresh air of
self-appreciation and genuine self-awareness. Even if
your heart feels contracted when you first open yourself

to feeling it, you may find that the act of focusing your attention in your heart region will quickly generate a flow of emotional healing energy into your heart. Or it may take time and offer you a wonderful opportunity to learn to be patient, gentle, and accepting of yourself just as you are.

After reading this paragraph, sit quietly for a few minutes, or lie down if you want to, or even go for a stroll around the block, whatever feels right to you… Again tune into your breathing… feel how your breathing is intimately related to your heartbeat… relax your tongue and jaw… imagine that you're breathing deep down into your belly and pelvis… let your body relax and begin to feel good again… breathe through your mouth if you feel any emotional pressure inside you… and say to yourself a few times, "This is good, this is enough for right now"… Relax and accept whatever it is you are feeling….

CHAPTER FIVE

Moving Beyond Loss and Abandonment

Once you have established a heart connection through regular meditation and have begun to accept the feelings that arise in meditation, you are likely to find that memories of past unresolved hurts spontaneously come to you. We have all experienced emotional losses in our lives—relationships that didn't work out, the death of loved ones, early feelings of abandonment that have never been fully resolved. Often we have experienced all of these. The dynamic is essentially the same, whether we have more-or-less "recovered" from these losses or whether the pain is still immediate and present. In this chapter, we will be looking especially at dealing with emotional pain at its most intense, but with the understanding that it has roots in the pain that we inevitably experience as children.

Even if your own situation does not involve current feelings of loss, it will be useful to read this chapter and engage in the process of recovery I have outlined. Once you establish a heart connection with yourself, you can use this as an opportunity to explore and heal painful losses and separations that you never fully worked through. It is safe to say that virtually all of us carry old wounds that are not completely healed. These experiences can be so intense, especially if they happened when you were a child, that it is normal to numb yourself to the pain and go to any lengths to avoid experiencing it fully. If experiences of separation and abandonment are not fully resolved, they remain a lifelong obstacle to your loving relationship with yourself.

When we first enter a period of being alone, it is often the case that we are suffering from a painful separation from another person or our family. Or we may feel rejected and lonely, simply because we have always associated being alone with being abandoned. The pain we feel in our hearts when we feel abandoned, unloved, lonely, or rejected, is not just something that exists in our mind. Heartache is in fact a physiological condition involving actual muscular tensions in and around the heart, stimulated by a complex emotional/mental construct in the brain. Loneliness is a very real pain in our bodies.

To relieve this pain, we must go through a process that combines emotional, mental, and physiological release. I used the phrase "emotional healing" in the last chapter. This term quite accurately describes what happens when we let go of the constrictions that cause the pains of loneliness and recover our ability to feel good in our hearts.

When we feel abandoned, our first response is usually anger, which goes back to the early primal fear for our survival. This is obvious in little children who throw a fit of rage when they realize they have been left by their mother or father. Anger is a beautiful and powerful emotion of the human body, designed to provide energy for overcoming dangers or obstacles to our getting what we need. Quite often, children do get what they want (mommy or poppa back) by screaming bloody murder when left at the day-care center or with a baby-sitter.

But once we reach a certain age, angry outbursts do little good. And in fact, little children, when left alone or with a relative stranger, must go beyond rage and enter into the next phases of abandonment feelings—sorrow, hopelessness, depression, despair. These feelings are triggered by the fact that anger has not provided relief from the feelings of abandonment. Each of us as young children went through this progression from anger to despair, in which the heart feels powerful muscular contractions from which there is no relief.

And as we matured, we needed to learn how to endure this feeling and hopefully break free of its grip as quickly as possible.

If you have become solitary because your mate or best friend has died, because you have split up with your mate or lover, or you have had to leave your closest friend, the experience of suddenly being alone is almost always a heart-rending one. And there is no easy way around the pain of separation. The pain of separation or abandonment is created by the loss of the sense of unity between your heart and the heart of another person. The identification with that person is a matter more of the heart than of the head.

Although you may have been the one who initiated the separation, you are still likely to feel some degree of abandonment by the other person. Though it may seem illogical, it is part of the normal dynamics of separation, of breaking heart contact. Whatever the cause, when you are separated from heart contact with someone you love, your heart feels in fact rent in two. The union has been broken, and this break is extremely painful.

Over the years, what I have found in my own life experience, as well as in that of my therapy clients and my friends, has been this: when one runs out and immediately finds someone to take the place of the old love or friend, this new relationship is doomed to failure. A "rebound" relationship is not a solid relationship, but just an attempt to ease pain by substituting a new person for the one lost. The grafting process might temporarily ease the pangs of loneliness, but in the long run it interferes with emotional healing—and the new relationship explodes at some point, leaving us in worse shape than if we had faced our solitary condition honestly and alone.

If you are going through a process of heartbreak and recovery, how are you dealing with your situation? Are you trying to run away from your solitary condition, or are you accepting it? Do you accept what has happened to you, or are you rejecting the situation you are in? Are you willing to go through the emotional recovery process, or do you want to avoid it by jumping into a new relationship before you have recovered from your last one?

Take a breather from reading… tune into your heart… see how your heart feels right now… notice any feelings of contraction in the heart and breathing muscles… notice what happens when you try to accept your present condition… can you open yourself to the process of recovery?… breathe easily through your mouth… let your feelings move through you…

Since separation and emotional pain are something all of us have experienced early in life, you can go back in memory and look for the connection to your early life. In your present situation, you can become aware of the role of the past. You can become aware that your pain or lone-liness is not entirely *of* the present, that you are in part reacting to something that happened long ago, holding on—perhaps unconsciously—to an older attachment that set up a pattern that is still with you today.

Take a few more moments now to go back in your memory… what does your present situation remind you of?… what story are you replaying?…
Are you partly grieving from the pain of an older wound?… Breathe easily and gently… Allow space in your heart for your feelings to move through…

To accept and heal our wounds and move into emotional maturity is a challenge for all of us. We might think we are very mature, emotionally, but when the rug is pulled out from under us, we may find ourselves in the grip of emotions we have not experienced since we were young children. Opening to these childlike feelings is essential to recovery, because this pain always has deep roots in childhood experiences of abandonment.

To recover, we need to open ourselves quickly to the pain in our hearts, and to focus our attention in the direction of the pain rather than running away from it. It is important not only to experience the pain fully, but at the same time to use meditation to relax the muscular contractions that cause the pain in heart. The two go together, otherwise you are just repeating the pain and harming yourself further.

When we do consciously face our pain and begin the physical process of relaxing into it, we can progress through the letting-go process quickly. Since our normal survival reaction to pain is "fight or flight," relaxing into and accepting any kind of pain—physical or emotional—is something that must be consciously learned. In moving through the various stages of recovery, you need to be aware of this natural tendency to avoid pain and patiently allow yourself to experience it, with the confidence that you have the ability to move through and beyond it.

Another thing to be aware of is that frequently, when experiencing painful feelings, we find it hard to be loving to ourselves—it is the old childhood logic that if you are experiencing something bad, you must *be* bad yourself. You will need to take some time to offer reassurance to your wounded self that has fallen into this self-accusing state.

In the recovery process, dealing with anger toward those who have hurt us is a crucial step. We need to feel the anger honestly, admit the feeling of abandonment, and keep releasing the anger until it is gone.

Some of us have difficulty bringing our anger to the surface and are inclined to move directly to feelings of grief. We may have been conditioned to feel that it is dangerous or wrong to be angry—especialy if the person has died. But anger is there, buried in the mix of emotions, whether or not we are conscious of it or accept it, and you can learn to move through it.

First of all, let's deal with your anger at being abandoned. This feeling is quite irrational in most people. The anger is instinctive, as we have pointed out already. So your thinking mind is going to be of no value whatsoever in dealing with it. You cannot make it go away through any neat, logical realization. What you have to do is to feel the anger honestly, admit that you have been abandoned in one way or another, and blow off the anger until it is gone.

You will need to experiment with the process of feeling the anger directly in your heart region. It is this anger that in fact purges the clinging to the person you have lost. So see the anger as positive, not negative. It might feel bad, but it is cathartic. It will begin to cleanse your heart, which means making room for something new in your life: a loving friendship with yourself and the possibility of new relationships free from the contamination of past bitterness. Sometimes, I might mention, the same person will end up returning to re-enter your heart in a new way. The purging of anger and hurt is often a necessary transition before anything new can happen in a relationship.

The basic process for releasing anger is simple to learn and remember:

Give yourself a few minutes when you can be alone and undisturbed. First tune into your breathing... notice how you feel when you think of the person you are separated from... allow youself to feel the muscular contractions in and around your heart as you breathe... open your mouth and breathe into your feelings... allow your voice to make any sounds that want to come out of you to express your anger at the person who has left you, or at yourself for leaving this person...

Allow words to express your anger... If you can comfortably do this, allow yourself to hit a pillow while you make sounds... When your anger has exhausted itself for the present, sit quietly and allow your breathing to slow, feel a relaxation, a release in your whole body...

Usually you will need to return to this process. Once you have done it, you'll know when anger begins to build up again. If your anger is not easily available to you, be patient with yourself. It will be useful to return to the technique after you have made some progress in releasing other feelings. You can't set a timetable for progress—everything comes in its own time.

The next phase after releasing anger is to move into grieving and acceptance. This is a gentler experience than emotional release related to anger. Crying is the physiological vehicle for discharging the emotional and physiological tensions in the heart in this stage of recovery—even if the emotional trauma is a very old one that you are working through years later. This surrender to feelings that you may think of as childish is necessary to a rapid, successful recovery. It means, until the pain is resolved, you will need to retreat to a private place where you can cry. Once you feel you have moved through your anger, do the following meditation:

Take a break to breathe into your feelings... Put the book aside... breathe through your mouth to let your feelings come out... notice what happens when you think about your loss and the person you are separated from... notice any tension in your throat and begin to relax into the crying reflex if you are ready...

Emotional maturity requires the willingness to admit one's losses and go through the process of emotional discharge and healing. Maturity refers to a certain wisdom, a certain understanding of how you do heal emotionally. It refers to the realization that time heals old wounds if we surrender to the natural process of emotional recovery. Maturity means keeping a certain sense of perspective, knowing that the painful phase will pass and better times will come again.

Recovery from old or recent emotional wounds takes us through a definite death and rebirth into a new period in our lives. The old unity does die. This is the reality of loss. I knew an old man who lived with his dog, and one day the dog died, after some years of providing faithful companionship. The old man went through the same emotional trauma and death-rebirth as he did fifteen yeas before, when his wife died. Love is love. After the loss comes the recovery process and rebirth into a new relationship with yourself, as well as readiness for new friendships.

In the recovery process, as you work through recent losses and re-experience and let go of old, under-lying traumas, you will find an expansiveness in your heart that you may never have experienced before, and a deeper appreciation of your solitary spirit.

CHAPTER SIX

Reviewing Your Life Patterns

Each new day brings with it a wide assortment of emotional ups and downs, ins and outs, highs and lows. As our thoughts meander through the morning, the afternoon, the evening, and into the night, they stimulate a host of associated emotions within us. And these emotions in turn stimulate thoughts related to the feelings. Sometimes we might feel lonely, but at other times we might feel very good within our hearts and relish the experience of solitude.

As you move through the processes in this book, it is useful to review your patterns of relating to solitude as well as relating with other people. In reading the statements below, you will get a sense of how your attitudes, feelings, and habits concerning solitude may have changed. Notice which statements best reflect your feelings at present:

1) I try to avoid how I feel, because usually when I look inside me, I find emotional pain and contraction.

2) Sometimes when I'm alone with myself these days, I feel lonely, and sometimes when alone, I feel at least a little expansion and good feelings in my heart.

3) Now and then I am gripped with the feelings of loneliness, but mostly I'm feeling quite good when alone.

4) I'm mostly over lonely feelings, and enjoy being alone with myself, as long as I'm socializing enough in between.

5) I'm not sure how I feel when alone for very long, because I try to avoid being alone altogether.

6) Even when I'm alone, I busy myself with projects and plans, memories and fantasies, so that I don't have to come into contact with the feeling of being alone.

Each of us establishes routines that dictate what we do, day to day. It is important to gain some sense of perspective on these habits so that they can be altered if they severely limit our opportunities for encountering ourselves in solitary situations. It is a great sorrow, a tragedy of life, when people bury themselves in patterns of behavior that deny them access to their own solitary presence.

When we have been conditioned by pain over and over again, so that we avoid the situation where pain occurred in the past, then we are held prisoner to past events. We are not free to move into the newness of the present moment. Most of us, most of the time, are in fact prisoners of such conditioning. We lead limited lives, not venturing into realms of consciousness or activity that have in the past led to emotional or physical pain and upset. In order to change this programming fundamentally, we need to do inner work, such as I've described in earlier chapters, to release and move beyond the pain. But we can also make conscious choices that will help to change the limiting patterns we observe in our lives.

To do this we need to assess our daily habits, both mental and behavioral, to see how we have been conditioned, and to see where we need to expand our lives in positive directions. Let's consider patterns in three areas that will help you identify some changes you may want to make in your life:

First of all, consider your interpersonal habits. Are you someone who keeps very much to your established set of friends and associates, or do you regularly open yourself to make contact with new people, with relative strangers? Have you contracted into a tight, secure circle of friends, perhaps dropped away from close friendships altogether, or are you open to encounters with new personalities, with new influences in your life?... Pause, close your eyes perhaps, and let these interpersonal questions resonate within you until you have an honest assessment of your present interpersonal habits...

When you have the choice of being alone with yourself for an hour or two, or of socializing, which do you usually choose? Do you almost always escape from solitary encounters with yourself by choosing to be in a social situation? Or do you regularly choose the solitary path, so that there is ample opportunity for you to be quietly alone with yourself, enjoying your own company, working through internal traumas, and getting to know your deeper self, better?... Pause again, put the book aside, reflect on your habits...

When you do find yourself alone, what are your normal habits? Do you quickly lose yourself in head-tripping, indulging in cognitive activity to the exclusion of perceptual and emotional experiencing? Do you busy yourself with habitual tasks which give you no time to quietly look inward to see how you are feeling at the moment? Do you compulsively get involved in one problem-solving activity after another so that you are lost to your physical presence? Or do you in fact regularly just pause, relax, say hello to yourself, and nurture your friendship with your inner presence?… Take a few moments to put the book aside, pause, and reflect on these questions…

I would suggest that you take these three areas of your life and get to know yourself within their parameters very well, indeed. Honesty is crucial. Begin to develop a new, more inclusive, more honest image of yourself in the present moment, so that you have a clear understanding of how you are programmed to run your life. Only by seeing the programming, as I have said already, do you put yourself in position to alter it for the better.

When you finally see what you are doing with your life out of habit, then you can change that habit. Seeing clearly is the first step. And very often, the act of seeing is itself the initiator of positive evolution in your lifestyle. To see a danger allows you instantly to respond with action that moves you away from the danger. If you see a tree starting to fall in your direction, the very act of seeing the tree falling toward you stimulates a powerful reaction in your body to escape.

It is the same way with emotional danger. When you see that you are doing something that is severely limiting your enjoyment of life, hampering your recovery from an emotional contraction, damaging your relationship both with yourself and others, then the seeing of this habit does generate an emotional movement away from it. This is the true beauty of the human personality, of the human progression through life. We naturally evolve in directions that seem to improve our life situation, if we are willing to look honestly and unblinkingly at our present situation. This tendency to move in the direction of healthy habits is a powerful evolutionary force, since life involves so many experiences which generate contractions and inhibitions.

But certain habits are likely to become set in our personalities because of programming that makes us afraid to look honestly at the habit itself. When this is the case, then we do have difficulty in recovering from old emotional wounds and moving forward in life.

Abandonment is one experience that can deprive us of a sense of perspective on our habits and contractions. Feeling abandoned is such a primal contraction that we have little cognitive perspective on the experience when it comes to us. And the emotional pain is so great that we have little ability to reflect on the feelings as they hold us in their grip. This is why recovery is so often incomplete, or distorted into defensive patterns of behavior. If you are experiencing a period of intense emotional trauma, it is important to concentrate on the healing processes outlined earlier in the book, especially in Chapter 5. When you have achieved some relief and feel like moving on, you will be better able to assess existing habits related to how you deal with opportunities to be alone with yourself, as well as your dominant relationship patterns with others.

In assessing your present habits, give yourself time to look at them from all perspectives:

Take time to think logically about each of your habits... In what ways do they enhance your life?... In what ways do they limit it?... As you pause to tune in to your breath, look into memories that show your habits at work in the past... Imagine how you might change certain habits... Open your mind to intuitive insights about your overall personality and how it might evolve in positive directions... Remember to stay tuned in to your body, breathing easily, naturally, so that your emotions are free to take you where they will...

CHAPTER SEVEN

Balancing Your New Life

Solitude may be a temporary condition for you, or a deliberate choice, or a phase of life that you view as long-term. Whatever your circumstances, the important thing is to take solitude for what it actually is: not a rest period from social involvement, not a retreat from life, not a periodic necessary evil, not a way to pass time until something better comes along. Whatever the reasons for finding yourself alone, solitude is not a substitute mode of life: at this point in time, it *IS* your life—just as every moment in the past has been your life.

Whether or not solitude is your first choice, it may offer you a unique opportunity to build your life according to your own choices, perhaps to follow interests and inclinations you have had to shelve because of responsibilities to others. How many times have you said to yourself, "I have always wanted to...," and thought of a special unrealized ambition or interest. This may be the time to risk exploring that cherished wish in some way. Or this may be the time to develop some part of yourself, of your relationship to life, where you have felt a lack.

In a weekend seminar I gave recently, there were two men about my age who were quite different from the rest of the group in that they would almost certainly be dead within a few months. One of them had cancer of the lungs, the other cancer of the intestines. With remarkable courage, they were exploring ways to open and expand their personalities, at this late date in their lives.

These two men shared their feelings about what it was like to know that, barring a medical miracle, they would be gone from their bodies and this planet in such a short time. One of them told us something that stuck strongly in my mind. He commented that his primary sadness was that he had not taken the time to get to know himself better in his life. Now with the presence of his own demise so close over his shoulder, he could look back and see how he had focused hardly any attention on exploring his own inner realms of consciousness. And with the time he had left, that was exactly what he was doing—learning ways to open up his mind and heart to experience the deeper dimensions of being a human being.

The other fellow had a very different wish. He said he had been so caught up in his own little world all his life, that he had failed to open himself fully to experience other people and the world around him. He came to my seminar seeking rapid techniques for breaking free of his emotional and perceptual inhibitions so he could immerse himself as much as possible in the world around him before he died.

Actually, what both of these brave men were expressing was in fact the same basic desire. They wanted to expand that polarity of inner and outer, that continuum between our innermost center and the furthest reaches of our perceptual environment. To participate fully in this continuum is in fact to live life to the utmost. If we retreat entirely into our inner realms, we become neurotic, imbalanced, out of touch with life. And to ignore our inner solitary spaces equally cuts off the possibility of the two polarities creating a vital flow of energy through our beings.

These men also provide a reminder that, as I mentioned above, this is life itself, and we don't have time to wait around for something better to happen.

Throughout this book, we have spoken about the inner/outer polarity in terms of self-relationship versus relationship with others, and about achieving a healthy balance in this area. We have also talked about overcoming the negative self-judgment process that limits our ability to have good relationships with ourselves and others. We have not yet looked at balancing the more general ways in which our consciousness functions.

We can roughly identify the four modes of consciousness as follows: First there is the thinking, or cognitive mode, which involves processing and judging information and acquiring knowledge. Second, there is sensation, which consists of sensory inputs from both inside and outside the body. Thirdly, emotions are a neurophysical response of the body/mind to thoughts and sensations. The fourth mode, intuition, is a kind of direct knowing that seems to come to us mysteriously. Without getting involved in complex theories of the human mind and brain, we can identify the basic ways our consciousness functions: thinking, sensing, feeling, and intuiting.

To create a lifestyle in which these elements are balanced, we first need to examine just what our patterns are and what types of conscious experience we find ourselves habitually drawn to. Then we need to add balance by enriching our days with the kinds of experience we may have been starved for, and reducing those that may be limiting our growth and dampening our spirits. We go through life, often conditioned by these patterns in our early years, and may not realize that our lives are not in balance. So it may require careful self-observation—such as I've recommended elsewhere in this book—to know exactly what your patterns are in each area. Solitude can help this process along. Each of these forms of consciousness can be experienced either in social settings or in solitary settings. But we are most able, consciously, to observe and develop these functions of the mind when we are alone and not having to deal with social interaction at the same time. Solitary space allows us to experiment with satisfying combinations of experience that will enrich our own solitary lives and enhance our enjoyment of social situations, as well.

Let us consider each function in terms of the daily patterns of life.

THE THINKING MODE

If at times it seems that I devalue the thinking function of the mind, it is because almost every one of us in contemporary society has been trained to over-value cognitive thinking. In school, especially, we are rewarded for fixating on cognitive activity, to the exclusion of the other three factors in a well-balanced personality.

However, to go in the opposite extreme and negate our cognitive life would be pure foolishness, as well. We have remarkable minds, and we should in fact spend regular time enriching this dimension of personality so that we can think clearly about our lives, communicate deeply with other people, and make conscious decisions about what is most important to do in our lives. Cognitive information is also an important window to the wider world and helps us become more aware of our connections with humanity and the planet itself.

Consider your own daily routines of consciousness. Your patterns of work, for example, may keep you in an information-processing mode for many hours of the day. Do you balance this with sensory experiences when you come home from work, or do you reach for the newspaper? Or does your work provide little or no intellectual stimulation? Are you starved for information from the wider world? There is also the issue of which mode you trust or depend on most habitually. Given your educational conditioning, do you place most trust in your analytical, judgmental powers to define what is real? Are you willing to relax into sensory experience? Can you trust yourself to give free reign to feelings? Are you willing to trust intuitions that come to you without the credentials of logic?

Take a few moments to tune in to your breath and

quietly get a sense of what your consciousness is like most of the time... do you return again and again to analyzing, trying to figure things out, as the way to guide yourself in your life?... Do you experience yourself trying to resolve problems by running mentally around the same tracks over and over?... Are you always hungry for information—brain food?... Do you use your thinking mind in a responsive, expansive way that opens you to your connection with the wider world and to deeper understanding of yourself?... Do you neglect other kinds of experience; sensory, emotional, intuitive?... As you let these questions resonate within you, notice what you are feeling in your body... your level of comfort or discomfort... Your body will let you know if there is an imbalance... Listen to your body... What do you sense may be neglected in the patterns of your daily life?...

A primary source of vitality in our thinking is often overlooked. This source is the amount and quality of new sensory inputs we take into our minds. In order to advance intellectually, we must regularly enrich our supply of images and experiences from which new thoughts, concepts, and perspectives can develop.

So if you want to optimize your cognitive development, it is essential that you consciously observe your habits of thinking versus your habits of tuning into sensory experience. Sensory or perceptual inputs are the food that provide the building blocks of growing concepts. Do you feed yourself adequately, or are your thoughts impoverished and malnourished because of certain limiting mental habits? To answer this question, we now need to consider the dimension of sensation, or perception, in your everyday life.

SENSATION

Our minds are certainly pre-programmed considerably with genetic patterns for making sense of the world around us and our position in the world. But only through the input of a vast amount of perceptual information as we grow up does this genetic programming receive the stimulation and guidance needed for the mind to form functional concepts of how to succeed in life.

We have our five senses, and perhaps some more subtle ones as well, that are in fact antennas for receiving information about the world around us and our own internal states. The brain receives this information and then goes to work processing it. In other words, perception moves into cognition as sensory

inputs are digested by the mind and ultimately trans-
formed into images, memory, and concepts based on
these images and memories. Thus we become thinking
beings as we transform raw perceptual information
into symbolic sense.

Unfortunately, early in our lives many of us
quickly fixate on the thought patterns we have learned
in our struggle to survive and mature. These patterns
are interpretations of reality that enable us to navigate
through life and understand it, to a degree. As such, they
become exclusive—they cause us to block out new perceptual experiences that might threaten these safe attitudes and belief systems. Our minds become rigid. We
can easily become insensitive, unresponsive to the
changing world around us, and limit our own inner
development, as well. If this happens, we turn into
modern-day dinosaurs, unable to keep up with the
changing times, and thus losing touch.

Many people who find themselves unable to reach
out and make new friendships are suffering from this
calcification of their conceptual minds. They have in
fact dropped away from the cutting edge of the present
moment and have slipped into an internal bubble of
attitudes and judgments that insulate them from
encounters with the outside world.

An intense preoccupation with cognitive mental activity may not bring social isolation—if there are friends of a similar disposition. But to the extent that it displaces other modes of consciousness, it will interfere with the development of intimacy, both in one's self-relationship and in one's relationships with others. Since sensation, emotion, and intuition are fundamental aspects of our personality, neglecting these experiences prevents us from knowing ourself on a deep level.

If you tend to isolate yourself—internally or externally—from the full range of sensory experience, it will take conscious effort to begin shifting your attention away from thinking, analyzing, and judging, and toward the actual sensory experiences coming to you every moment of your life. If you do the following meditation faithfully, as often during the day as possible, you will gradually sense in yourself a greater inner freedom as you participate more fully in the sensory experience of life.

The meditation begins like the earlier ones... You are sitting comfortably, tuning into your breathing... Breath is the key to awakening perceptual consciousness ... feel the sensation of air flowing in... then out... Feel the movement of your body as you breathe in... out... Close your eyes... Notice whether you can feel your heartbeat or your pulse somewhere in your body, without any effort… (sometimes you may not feel your pulse at first… each person is different)… Expand your awareness to include your sense of sitting upright… notice which muscles are keeping you upright… which are relaxed… notice how you are connected to the earth, rooted by the earth's gravity… Let your awareness move through your whole body, from your head to your fingers and toes… Leaving your eyes closed, expand your awareness to include the sounds you hear around you, background sounds, and sounds that come and go… Notice any odors in the air… and whether the air is warm or cool, and how it feels on your skin… Feel the pressure against your body as you sit on a chair or couch or on the floor, feel your feet on the floor… Reach out with your fingers to touch whatever is around you, or your own skin… feel the texture… Notice the taste in your mouth… eat something if you wish… Stay aware of your breathing and your whole body here in the present moment and all the sensations that come to you… When you feel ready, allow your eyes to open and look around… take in the powerful experience of visual stimulation as the outside world enters you, perceptually…

This basic sensory-awakening exercise will help you develop the habit of consciously opening yourself to the present moment, through your sensory organs. To experience the present moment, it seems that we need to be in touch with our senses in one way or another. If you want to interact fully, both with your own body and with the world around you, you will want to emphasize this sensory dimension of your own mind.

Pure sensory experiences as they enter your mind will, in turn, naturally stimulate the flow of thoughts. These new perceptions will also be stored in memory, and resonate within your memory, to stimulate new conceptual activity. This creative process is the magic dynamic of human perceptions and thought. In developing your relationship with yourself, this creative dynamic is the focal point, because you are in fact an integral part of this perceptual, sensory interaction with the outside world. You are not an isolated entity. In fact, the chracteristics of your self—your personality—come primarily from your vast storehouse of perceptual memories of the outside world.

EMOTION

But we are not simply perceivers and thinkers. We are emotional beings. Our emotions are programmed

into our genes. Babies are born with feelings, very powerful ones which help them to survive from day one in
life. And these feelings are developed through interaction with the outside world, so that perceptions stimulate emotional responses, and thoughts stimulate emotional responses, as well. Then the emotions stimulate
more thoughts, and a circular interaction of thoughts,
perceptions, and emotions is created.

In fact, we live within this interactive system all our
lives, with the balance moving somewhat in one direction or the other, but always based on the interplay of
feelings, sensations, and mental activity. Some of us
become overly fixated on our emotional dimension of
existence, while others of us try to avoid feelings altogether by fixating on thoughts or sensations, or both.

Within the realm of emotions there is also the need
for balance. Sometimes we become fixated on one or two
emotions, and habitually think thoughts that direct our
perceptions in such a way as to stimulate these emotions.
Some people try to feel happy all the time and to avoid
the darker emotions through being positive-minded, for
instance, and only seeing what they perceive as the good
in life. Other people fixate on chronic thoughts and feel
ings of worry and anxiety. Still other people fixate on
guilt feelings and self-deprecation.

If you tend to be dominated by one or two chronic emotional states, it is important to act consciously to break free of such habits so that you are able to respond spontaneously with the appropriate emotion in new situations. The principal emotions in the human repertoire are bliss or joy, anger, love, anguish, fear, playfulness, passion, grief, hopelessness or despair, mastery or confidence, repulsion, and serenity or peace. In your solitary reflections, it is strongly advisable to reflect on your openness to each of these basic emotional states and to see if you can bring a healthy balance into your life by regularly opening yourself to each of these feelings.

Beginning with the basic breathing/body meditation, meditate one by one on particular emotional patterns that do not seem to serve you.

Take a few moments now to tune into your breathing... and your awareness of your whole body... Think of any emotional pattern that you know limits your enjoyment of life... To begin with, simply look at it as a habit, like any other... Then notice what triggers it... some belief about yourself or others... some type of negative situation that always pushes your buttons... something that frustrates you in creating what you want in your life... Think of the last time this pattern occurred… remember what happened and breathe gently through it… notice what thoughts keep coming up… keep breathing through it… Move yourself away from what is happening, watch it from a distance… keep breathing through it… Notice any new thoughts, insights, feelings that come up…

In doing this type of meditation, you will become more aware of the impact these patterns have on your life and how they are triggered. The meditation itself can also help you begin to change your relationship to a particular pattern. Seeing it from a little distance, with more perspective, you may find that you give less energy to it, that more appropriate responses are available to you.

If the pattern is very ingrained and painful, you may want to return to earlier meditations in the book that help you explore the sources of particular patterns and ways to release them.

INTUITION

Thus far, we have seen how thinking, sensation, and feelings are not really separate entities, but in fact are part of the whole process of consciousness. There is a fourth dimension of consciousness which is crucial to personal growth and self-realization. Usually we use the word "intuitive insight" to reflect this functioning of the mind. Sometimes, in more spiritual terms, it is thought of as a flash of enlightenment. Whatever labels we use, we all know what it feels like to have a sudden insight, a sudden realization, knowledge, or answer that springs up spontaneously in our consciousness.

It seems that when all three of the first dimensions of consciousness are integrated and balanced, the mind can readily move into an expanded state of awareness in which linear, logical thinking is put aside in favor of a more comprehensive functioning. And in this expanded state of consciousness, intuitive insight happens instantaneously. All of us value this form of mental functioning but, in fact, few of us understand how to activate it. And the truth is that intuition cannot be pushed into action. It is an effortless phenomenon of the mind, coming to us when we surrender to it.

One of the main values of solitary reflection, of quiet retreat from social interaction, is the nurturing of the intuitive dimension of the personality. We spend much of our time using our minds to solve problems, get work done, communicate our thoughts and expectations to other people. Only when we take a break from our habitual patterns of everyday life do we put ourselves in position to relax the usual buzz of our minds so that in the midst of quiet reflection and contemplation, insights can come to us.

So, solitary times are of great value for gaining a new perspective on our lives through intuitive expansion of consciousness. In general, the meditations in this book will help you develop your intuitive faculty because they focus primarily on emptying the mind through connecting with the breath and body. Let me give you an additional reflective technique which will help you develop the inner freedom from interference by the thinking mind that is needed to open the intuitive dimension.

Again, tune into your breathing… your heartbeat and pulse… your whole body here in the present moment… your sense of grounding in the earth's gravity… your perceptions of the world around you through your five senses… And when you reach this expanded state of consciousness through full awareness of your senses, your breathing, your body, drop any expectations or preconceptions you may have about what your intuition might bring you… drop the desire to get or achieve anything… and begin to observe the flow of your mind… Notice feeling states that come and go… notices images and thoughts that flow through your mind effortlessly…

Return to this meditation, allowing yourself to become comfortable with it. Your thinking mind may want to program you to get particular information or demand specific answers from the deeper level of the mind. This will initially block the intuitive response. Once you have developed a relationship with this aspect of your mind, however, through practice and through respecting the way it functions, you will be able to present it with a subject you'd like more information on at the beginning of the meditation. This will be effective only if the subject or request is not presented as a demand but as a respectful request for help. If you are not used to opening yourself to intuition, you will need to be extremely patient. The intuitive faculty cannot be rushed or forced.

In balancing our lives in times of solitude, we need to come to terms with the fact that one source of pleasure that we once probably counted on—the society of other people—is less available than it once was. This does not mean that there is necessarily less pleasure in our lives, but we may have to be more imaginative and resourceful to find as much pleasure as we need. You have begun to look at the different aspects of consciousness and how to balance them in order to know yourself more fully and experience more of what life has to offer. But have you made enough room for pleasure in that balance?

In many families, an unspoken law of "pleasure last"—or pleasure not at all—has been the rule. Duty to others may come first. Work is a high priority, and you may have been conditioned throughout your adult life to base your self-worth on achievement in work. Denying yourself and cultivating unselfishness is, as I have mentioned before, an ideal many of us were conditioned to uphold. And pleasure, especially sensual pleasure, especially when alone, was very likely a prominent "don't." Too often, it has not been understood that pleasure is not inherently frivolous or inferior to some of the grimmer, more somber aspects of life; that it is central to creativity, to our connection with the world, to love of self and others. The first challenge is to deal with and transcend, through meditation, any negative feelings you may have about pleasure, as such. Begin by saying to yourself a few times, "I give myself permission to experience all kinds of pleasure," and see how the sentence feels to you as you say it. You may want to go back through some of the earlier chapters in this book to identify the source of any guilt associated with pleasure and then to release it.

Living alone, you need to realize that pleasure has an especially high priority for you in terms of your health and state of mind. One of the most rewarding experiences of solitude is to learn how to fill your life with many kinds of pleasures—pleasures of the mind, pleasures of the body, pleasures of the spirit. Allowing yourself pleasure is crucial to your self-relationship, to being your own best friend. Take a little time to reflect on pleasures that can enrich your life.

Again tune into your breath and your whole body… into all your senses… Remember some of the simple things that you enjoy every day… think of simple things that you would enjoy more if you took more time to notice them… think of activities you enjoy… friends you see now and then and whose company you enjoy… think of places you like… think of possessions that are like old friends to you… think of books or stories or poems that open the wide world to your imagination… think of the pleasure of your own presence… think of everything in your life that you are grateful for…

CHAPTER EIGHT

Developing Your Spiritual Awareness

Living with yourself can sometimes mean living completely alone for a prolonged period of time, sharing
space—but not your life—with other people, or sharing
your life but reserving time alone to devote attention to
your relationship with yourself. In any of these situations, a question arises: do you nurture or avoid nurturing your own spiritual development?

Spiritual development, as I use the term, is not
something separate from other dimensions of life. It
seems clear that each of us does have an indwelling spiritual presence that lies beyond our conceptual and emotional realms of experience, and yet exists nonetheless.
If we quietly open ourselves on a regular basis to self-
reflection, sooner or later we come into contact with
what I would call the spiritual core of our personality. It
is obvious that when we are alone, life itself presents
many more opportunities for spiritual awareness than it
would otherwise. In fact, for many people who are
alone, spiritual awareness is a primary means of con-

tacting joy in life. Thus, any discussion of solitary life needs to speak directly to the question of the spirit.

All religions are founded on the recognition of a spiritual dimension in human beings. But religions are social organizations, and often political and economic organizations, as well. They are group phenomena, not solitary phenomena. They often try to dictate what a person should experience when alone, but ultimately it benefits each of us to move beyond the guidelines of religious doctrines and take an honest look directly at this indwelling spirit that we experience when we quiet our minds and open our hearts to our own deeper presence.

In Christian terms, such reflection on spiritual levels is called contemplative prayer; in other religions the terms usually used are meditation, or in some instances, yoga. Whatever word is used, the aim is to transcend conceptual, logical, linear functions of the mind, and to listen directly to one's spiritual center—this may, depending on the belief system, be viewed as listening to God. Sometimes contemplative prayer or meditation is described as a reflective period when we stop asking God for something, and simply open ourselves to see what God might have to say to us. And for those of us who do not think in explicitly religious terms, we may speak of quieting the interior dialogue so that we can tune into non-programmed experiences which come to us directly, in the middle of the ongoing eternal present moment.

Whatever one's spiritual or religious preference, what matters is the regular pausing to quiet the mind so that communion with one's innermost spirit can take place. Religions are a function of cognitive beliefs and attitudes within the confines of a particular cultural understanding. Spiritual experience lies beyond such cognitive activity of the brain and focuses on direct, non-verbal experience.

It of course requires a certain trust in ourselves and in human nature if we are going to put aside our attitudes and beliefs about the nature of life and tune into the more direct experience of reality that lies beyond our conceptual mind states. Many people have been pro-grammed to fear that some evil force in the universe will immediately take their minds over if they relax and open themselves to a deeper experience of their own nature. Much of western religion is associated with a strong ten-dency to condition people to believe that their basic human nature is in fact sinful, evil, or untrustworthy.

If this is your belief, then you have two choices. You can avoid ever tuning into your deeper spiritual nature, and avoid the possibility that some evil force may take over your soul. Or, asking for guidance from God, you meditate to achieve a glimpse into your own spiritual center, to experience for yourself, your spiritual nature. The choice is always a personal decision for each of us.

For those of you who do want to look into your own spiritual nature, let me offer some basic meditation exercises which should prove valuable.

The first challenge, universally, is to quiet the thinking mind, which at first will feel threatened by the notion of being placed—even temporarily—in a secondary role. We have been taught from our earliest years that thinking is dominant, that reason is king, that using the cognitive center to control emotional and impulsive urges is necessary to our very survival. We are programmed with these underlying attitudes early in childhood.

So when I suggest that you regularly use your solitary times to quiet your thinking mind, your thinking mind may throw a dozen plausible reasons at you for never committing this seemingly heretical act. Who would you be, after all, without your thoughts? How would you in fact judge the experiences that might come to you, if you have turned off the judgmental part of your mind?

This of course is exactly the point. We do fear

entering realms of consciousness where judgment is silenced, where our ability to discriminate is shut off. We have based our entire survival on discrimination of good and bad, better and worse, helpful and dangerous. What would happen if we lost this judgmental ability in the midst of exploring our deeper spiritual self? Our continual thinking serves a defensive function, which is to keep us from experiencing our solitary self in the present moment.

We find ourselves back to the question we were asking earlier: are we our own best friends? And what does "best friend" mean? Do we really accept and love our deeper selves, or are we distrustful of who we really are? Do we accept our human nature as it is, or have we been programmed to turn against even our own being and to trust only influences that come from outside us?

My suggestion is this: begin to look tentatively in the direction of your own inner center. Explore for yourself who you really are, beyond all your education and cultural conditioning. This is one of the best uses for solitude, and can be a primary means for enriching your life.

How does one quiet the thinking mind? Thoughts seem to flow through our minds almost without a break. We are thinking beings, or so it seems, and we have made a god of thinking. Theology is the act of thinking about God, after all. And we tend to base our religious convictions on theological premises rather than direct experience, which means that we have religions that are thought-deep. We have seen in previous chapters that our "spontaneous" thought patterns are nothing more than conceptual programming inherited from our cultural background, interacting with our perceptual experiences in life.

The question is how to turn off thoughts, to quiet the internal dialogue. There are some very demanding meditative techniques for doing this, and also some quite simple ones. It is better to stick with the simple ones unless you are interested in devoting much of your life to rigorous spiritual discipline.

One of the best psychological techniques for quieting the flow of thoughts is to simply give the thinking mind something worthwhile to do, in the midst of meditation. Instead of trying to kill off your cognitive mind, let your cognitive mind participate in the meditation experience. This is a technique used throughout the world in religious training. Catholics use simple repeated prayers to silence the flow of normal thoughts through the mind. Hindus and Buddhists and Moslems use mantras, chanting, or prayers for the same purpose.

Traditional cultures such as the Hopi Indians in America, the Basutu in Africa, and other tribal groups also use chants and internal mantras to quiet the mind and prepare the person for direct contact with the divine.

The saying of a mantra or religious phrase or prayer is, in part, a breathing exercise. We speak on the exhales and are silent during the inhales. Breath and mantra are unified. The awareness of breathing that you have practiced in each reflection and memory exercise in this book can be directly put to use in spiritual exploration.

The most basic spiritual meditation of all is this: as you breathe, count your breaths. Keep your mind busy thinking the numbers in conjunction with watching your breathing. You can count up higher and higher if you enjoy that experience. Or you can count up to ten or twelve or any other number you choose, and then count down again to zero. Or you can begin again without counting down to zero. The particular structure you use is not crucial.

One of the most important things to remember before beginning any meditation practice is, as I've indicated before, that the thinking mind has a stake in staying in charge. You need to approach meditation with a gentle, accepting attitude toward yourself and what you will experience. At some point, probably many many times, the thinking mind will resist you in various ways. You will find that your attention has strayed from the meditation and you are thinking about something quite different. Your thinking mind may come up with all sorts of distracting concerns—from plans for tomorrow to present physical tensions. Or it may slide into dream images—you may even fall asleep. The important thing is not to give in to self-judgment and discouragement, but to persist, remembering that you have put some effort into becoming your own best friend and this is a chance to demonstrate that friendship. Don't lose sight of that in meditation. Also discard expectations, ideas of what should happen in meditation. You can't know what you will experience. Don't compare yourself with someone you know who has meditated. Drop any preconceptions—including those you may pick up by reading this book!

In counting your breaths, what happens most often is this: eventually the thinking mind will get tired of counting and will fall silent, though there is still awareness of the breath, coming in, going out. Sometimes this happens fairly quickly; at other times it takes longer. People are different, and your own state of mind will vary each time you sit down to meditate. But it gets better; the thinking mind learns that a little rest is not a catastrophe.

When the thinking mind falls silent, you will enter into a state of expanded spiritual awareness which lies at the heart of solitude. You will be quietly with yourself, quietly focused on your breathing, and thus your entire body. You breathe air that is coming from the outside world and thus connecting you intimately with your environment. If you practice meditation faithfully and patiently, you will experience inside and outside as one— intuitively you will experience for yourself the wholeness and unity that are the underlying spiritual realities of life. If you stop participating in this wholeness, if you stop breathing just for a few minutes, you of course cease living altogether, end of story. So breathing is a natural path that leads you to the experience of oneness.

Take a few moments right now to review the last three paragraphs. If you know that you will not be interrupted, and if you are feeling calm and relaxed, it would be a good time to practice this meditation. Tune in to your breath, select a counting pattern (you can change it if you wish)… let all expectations fall away… and begin…

Beyond this basic meditation, there are of course infinite varieties to choose from. You may want to

explore some of the spiritual traditions that use meditation. Seek out meditation techniques that work for you,
as well as a group that has similar goals to your own, if
you're so inclined. But beware of religious traditions
that attempt to control your experience of your interior
spiritual being. There is much manipulation and programming done in the name of religion, as I am sure
you know. The most helpful guideline I have found is
this: first explore spiritual experience for yourself, in as
simple a manner as possible. Then see what religious
frameworks best reflect your actual experience. This
way, you begin with truth as you directly experience it.

It has always seemed to me that spiritual experience is nothing more than an expansion of intuitive
experience. The challenge is to relax the thinking mind
enough to allow that particular mode of brain function
to shut down for a short while so that the other, more
subtle modes of consciousness can finally have their
opportunity to reach your conscious attention.

Let me give you another meditation technique.
Although my description of it is drawn from the Zen
tradition of Japan (which originated in the Buddhist
and Taoist traditions of China), other mystical traditions incorporate this basic form of meditation. It combines the awareness of breath with awareness of some-

thing perceived in the outside world, but keeping the awareness also devotedly focused on breathing and visual perception.

If it appeals to you, take the opportunity to try this meditation now. You will be sitting quietly, indoors or outdoors, with a view of a natural scene such as a tree, a flower, a mountain. Or you can meditate indoors, perhaps focusing on a lighted candle. Choose something you'd like to spend time looking at… make sure it is aesthetically pleasing to you. First, close your eyes and tune your attention to your breathing… the sensation of the air flowing in and out your nose or mouth… the sensation of movement in your chest and belly as you breathe… then open your eyes and quietly look at the chosen view or object… let your mind think whatever thoughts it wants to, about the object you are looking at, with the request that your thoughts remain related to that object… keep your breathing central in your mind… keep your awareness of your whole body central as well… expand your awareness to include the visual experience in front of you… notice what happens… your thoughts may fade away… see what unique experience comes to you…

As I said at the beginning of the chapter, what I
mean by spirituality is not something separate from all
of life. Solitude gives you an extraordinary opportunity
to find out what spiritual awareness means for you,
personally. The calm, open state of meditation spills
into your daily life, bringing you into a different kind of
relationship with everything around you, and with
yourself, as well. When you are alone, and permitting
yourself to experience your own presence, meditation
begins to blend with daily life in surprising and
rewarding ways.

CHAPTER NINE:

Finding Happiness in Solitude: Three Personal Stories

A worried father came to my office one morning to talk about his ten-year-old boy. According to the father, his son Peter seemed to be suffering from some sort of social problem. He didn't like playing with other children. He went to school and did okay there but, after school and on weekends, he didn't want to get together with his schoolmates as "normal children" his age did. Instead, he liked playing alone most of the time—he even seemed to relish a whole weekend without a single playmate coming over or inviting him off to do the usual boy things.

The father was a quite gregarious man who came from a large family and was involved in the sales end of a business. Peter was his third child, and the other two boys, according to the father, were "quite normal" in their behavior. What could be done with Peter to "get him out of his shell," to get him into more normal social relating "before he becomes a total recluse?"

I agreed to meet with Peter, who came around to my office the next week, after school. He was uncomfortable in the presence of his huffing, concerned father, and so I asked to talk with the boy alone. We had a good chat for almost an hour. I asked him many questions, and he responded honestly though at times a little hesitantly. I couldn't detect any real problems except for his problem with his parents: they didn't accept him the way he wanted to be. They wanted him to be a way he just wasn't.

"It's fun, being home doing what I want," Peter said. He told me he liked to draw, play Game Boy, and play with his bird. He liked to read, and sometimes he played basketball with his big brother. "He's fun, he can tell really good jokes."

"What about your friends at school?" I asked.

"Oh, they're cool, most of them. School's cool."

"What about after school? Do you feel lonely at home, would you rather be out playing with some of your friends?"

"Oh, I don't like all the noise and the fighting and everything," he said. "It's dumb, most of it, and it's more fun reading and doing things at home."

As far as I could tell, this was a boy who just preferred his own company most of the time. He spent seven hours a day in the company of his peers at school. That was enough for him. I met with his parents the next morning, and told them my opinion. "Maybe later on he'll find friends he wants to be closer with," I said. "That often happens. But we should respect these kids who enjoy their own company. They seem to be as happy as people who need to have other people around to be happy."

Peter's parents were not pleased with my opinion, and they took the boy off to another therapist, who struggled to make him be more social—with what results, I never knew.

If we showed signs of preferring to be alone when we were children, we were very likely pressured to be social beings by our parents and peer group. Certainly, many children need help in overcoming social fears and relating comfortably in a group. But at the same time, it happens that children are judged to be "messed up" and "not normal" just because they have found the special blessing of enjoying their own company and being at peace without being in a group setting.

As I have stated earlier in this book, I believe we should nurture a child's capacity for being alone, just as much as we nurture the social instinct. For thousands of years, children in primitive settings undoubtedly had the opportunity to drift a little distance from the family group and be alone in nature, at peace in their solitary hearts. Nowadays, the daily opportunities for moments of solitude in a child's life are mostly shattered by the presence of television—that no-man's-land where we're not socializing but we're not alone, either. And for seven hours a day, five days a week, most children spend their days in school, forced to be in a group of up to thirty-five other children their own age—a much more unnatural situation than being alone.

Peter had discovered the magic of solitude in his early life. Then his parents and therapist pressured him to change. Probably, he learned to feel guilty, to feel that he wasn't quite OK, because he liked his own company so much. As an adult, he will probably have to work hard to get over negative self-judgment caused by his parents' and therapist's rejection of his natural predisposition to peace and quiet and alone times.

Let's not do this to our own children—and let's liberate ourselves from any judgments of this kind that were laid on us during our own childhood.

✦✦✦✦✦✦✦✦✦✦✦✦✦✦

Some years ago, on a trip down to Guatemala, I was high in the mountains near a beautiful lake called Lago Atitlan. Most of the inhabitants of this highland region are pure-blooded Indians, descendants of the ancient Maya. Here and there, however, I came across people from all over the world, living a simple life far from the bustle of contemporary society. I had been hiking alone all day around the west side of the lake (there being no road at all around half of the rugged shore), and came upon a small, isolated Indian village.

I asked if there was any kind of inn in the area. I was guided to the secluded house of an American woman who lived some distance from the village, up the banks of a rushing stream and across a couple of intensely farmed meadows. I knocked, and a woman of about fifty opened her door and invited me in. She was quiet, friendly, and obviously quite content inside her own skin, way out here in nowhere. She had a guest room she sometimes rented out for a night or a week. I took the room and her offer of dinner, and refreshed myself with a bracing cold shower since she had no hot water in the house.

Over a simple but very tasty dinner, I found myself relaxing effortlessly in her company. We didn't talk much; she didn't pry into my life or my reasons for being in Central America, and I didn't press her to tell her own story. After a bottle of wine and a honey dessert made by the wife of her caretaker, who lived nearby, she told me simply that she had come down here on vacation from Atlanta with her husband eleven years ago and had mysteriously "found her soul" in this place. She moved here, on her own, against the strong wishes of her husband and her family.

Most of the time, she said, she was alone here, except for the occasional person such as myself who would discover her haven for a few days, and then move on. Old friends still came down periodically, and that was nice. But usually she was alone, gardening, reading, reflecting, doing all the usual chores that make up domestic life rituals. "Sometimes, yes, I do get terribly lonely," she admitted. Then she would jump on the next bus down to the airport and fly back to Atlanta to stay for a few weeks. "But that soon enough becomes tiresome," she said. Back she would come, more than content to be just with herself again.

We went out onto her balcony. It overlooked the native gardens, where families were out working and laughing together in the late evening light of summer. "They're my family now," she said. Living on the edges of their community, she said, was enough human contact for her. "I just never much took to all the gabbing and hugging and social responsibilities up in the States. I'm much more content down here."

After a while she said it was bedtime for her, that she would be up at the crack of dawn since that was her favorite time of the day. And she left me sitting there watching the evening drift over the valley. A peace came over me which felt like the breath of God rising up the small canyon with the evening breeze. I ended up staying there for two weeks, feeling I'd found what I was looking for on that vacation trip—my own precious solitude.

* * * * * * * * * * * * * * * *

A friend of mine from Basel, Switzerland, has very realistically found solitude to be his best friend. Dieter was married once, from the age of twenty-two to thirty-one. The marriage ended in a rather amiable but necessary divorce. He is still friends with his ex-wife and close to his grown children, but his lifestyle is very definitely that of a man who has found peace with himself to such an extent that he's utterly content to live alone. For several years after his relationship with his wife fell apart, Dieter struggled to find a new relationship that would replace his marriage. He had a number of live-in girlfriends and almost married one of them. But somehow, again and again, he found himself backing out of a traditional long-term sexual relationship and dyad bonding involvement.

With each new love relationship, Dieter learned a little more about the ingrained cultural programming which was driving him from woman to woman. Following a particularly devastating break-up, he decided as a conscious act to take a breather from all intimate relating for six months, just to let the water clear and find out what he really wanted in life. He had a number of long-term friends in the publishing business, as well as extended family in the region. He was socially active, but at the age of thirty-seven he stopped slipping into the actions and emotions of romance which had dominated his life until then.

He rented a cottage in the Alps and retreated there most weekends, working on a book of his own, finally—and discovering just how much he enjoyed his own company! He suffered at first with pangs of loneliness, sure. But quite quickly, within weeks in fact, he found that he began to hunger for the weekend to come, when he could flee his busy business and social world in Basel, take the train two hours into the mountains, step off in his newfound village, buy some groceries at the local shop, and walk the half hour up to his isolated cabin.

He had dabbled in meditation all his adult life and

published quite a number of good books on the topic. Now, finally, he had the peace of mind and atmosphere to practice what he'd been preaching. Quickly, he found he had a quite strong hunger for more and more solitude and peace, deeper and deeper silence and inner reflection. As old romantic hungers and compulsions fell away, he discovered a sense of inner calm and clarity he'd never known existed before. And the more solitude he granted himself each week, the more he wanted.

Within a few months, Dieter shifted his workload so that he could leave on Thursday instead of Friday, and return on Monday morning rather than Sunday afternoon. His identity began to shift, as well, from being a very social to a more quiet man—and from being a city person to being more a lover of wide open vistas and people-less space. He also discovered the great pleasure of solitary walking and hiking, which he would do for several hours each day in the mountains, and for an hour each morning in Basel.

Naturally, his friends and family noticed this change come over Dieter, and some of them complained quite openly that he was neglecting his friendships and turning into a veritable recluse. They told him something must be wrong with him, that he should see a therapist and find out what was making him so anti-social.

His mother, in particular, was very worried about him, and sent her favorite pastor over to his house one evening to find out what was the matter.

"I told him quite clearly," Dieter said to me later, "that contrary to my mother's opinion, nothing at all was wrong with me. Quite the contrary. I was discovering a more satisfactory way to go about life, and opening, step by step, to a deeper encounter with God in the bargain."

Like a surprisingly large number of people who are just now beginning to come out of the proverbial closet with their supposedly anti-social preferences and predispositions, Dieter was discovering that his natural personality was a mostly solitary personality. He enjoyed his friends still, but he loved his solitude equally, if not more. And nothing his mother or anyone else could say would dissuade him from his new-found passion for living happily alone with himself.

"The atmosphere in a room with no one in it but me," he confided, "is entirely different than when I'm sharing space with someone else, such as you—no offense intended at all." He believed it was what would be experienced by anyone who had moved beyond the fears and pangs of loneliness to discover the magic of solitary life. "My thoughts soar," he told me. "My emotions become calm and a great peace can come into my soul. This is what life is all about, for me."

When I go to Europe, I very much enjoy stopping by to visit Dieter, who sometimes invites me up to his cottage in the Alps. Once, I stayed there while he was in Basel during the week, and I discovered for myself just how magical his solitary retreat could be. And when he returned on Thursday evening, we sat quietly together for over an hour, not talking, enjoying solitude together—the ultimate union of intimacy and privacy. It was a very spiritual sharing that occurred that evening. I'll never forget the feeling of being entirely within my own bubble of awareness, and at the same time sharing in an expanded bubble of peace that seemed to stretch out forever at that moment into the universe at large.

At some point, we looked into each other's eyes after gazing out over the meadowlands below his cottage. I could see he had truly found the deepest richness of the solitary life.

Preserving Solitary Space

Solitude is like an undeveloped plot of land in an other-wise over-developed region—it is where you can go to encounter feelings of wholeness. It provides you with the breath of fresh air that revitalizes your spirit. This is true whether you are living primarily alone or with other people. Solitary space, in which you can experience your own presence, also offers you a unique opportunity to contact your deeper self. In the same way that we are fighting to preserve natural parks and open space throughout our country, each of us needs to make an effort if we are to preserve personal solitary space within a culture that increasingly crowds our inner environment with distractions—with busyness, continual socializing, and vicarious experience via the media.

The principal force that can overcome this tendency to be distracted all the time is the strength of your friendship with your own self. To the extent that you value and enjoy your own company, you will want to maintain regular periods of retreat to be alone with your feelings, thoughts, perceptions, and the sense of your own presence. And to the extent that you do maintain this solitary space, you will strengthen your inner friendship.

After reading this book and working your way through the reflections and meditations, take a moment to consider the state of your relationship with yourself. Have you learned to value and enjoy being in your own presence? As you evolve toward a better relationship with yourself, it becomes important to consider how you will maintain the progress you have made.

You will need to look for specific ways of preserving your solitary space. Since most of us tend to be caught up in busyness, we need to take a personal inventory and look at where we may be overly social, where our schedules are too crowded with events, activities, and other habitual distractions. The next step is to look at where we can simplify our lives in order to leave time for our relationship with ourself.

Substantial blocks of time are important—hours, perhaps even days, of retreat refresh the spirit at a deep level. But many solitary breaks can be found in the space of a few breaths, perhaps when you look up from your work and stare off into the distance through an open window at the sky or clouds or trees, and tune into your breathing and the beauty of nature. A solitude break of at least four breaths is a healthy habit, not only for your self-relationship but for your total well-being, as has been recognized by researchers in the field.

In addition to the frequent short breaks—at least once an hour is recommended—we all need at least ten minutes, once a day, to get away from the house or office and be alone, totally away from the distractions of our lives. This means tuning into the breath and body, and completely letting go of the concerns of the day. It may mean resting or relaxing completely, or, alternatively, engaging in some form of exercise—either of which should be done alone. The important thing is to make it a habit.

Another way to strengthen your self-relationship and preserve solitary space is of course to continue with meditation and reflection on a daily basis. It has been my experience that in embarking on any program of personal growth, it is all too easy to slip back into old habits unless you return to the learning process over and over again. I have written this book with the intention of creating a manual that you can continue to work with over the long-term, rather than a one-time reading experience. It is my hope that you will go back over the text and do the meditations and reflections again and again, as a way to reinforce the foundation of your self-relationship. I hope that in doing so, you will reap the rewards that come with exploring the mysteries of your own being throughout your lifetime.

HEARTSFIRE BOOKS

Heartsfire celebrates spiritual evolution in the contemporary world with books that inspire growth and promote physical and spiritual healing. We are privileged to present original and compelling writers who speak from their hearts and guide us to the magic of everyday experience. If you have a manuscript that you feel is suitable for us, we would love to hear from you. Send a letter of inquiry to: *Acquisitions Editor*, **Heartsfire Books**, 500 N. Guadalupe Street, Suite G-465, Santa Fe, New Mexico 87501 USA. Email: heartsfirebooks@heartsfirebooks.com. Visit us at http://www.heartsfirebooks.com.

Heartsfire Consciousness Literature

Spirtuality for the Business Person:
Inner Practices for Success
Claude Saks
September 1998

The Alchemy of Love:
A Pilgrimage of Sacred Discovery
Robert Boldman

The Emerald Covenant:
Spiritual Rites of Passage
Michael E. Morgan

Fathers:
Transforming Your Relationship
John Selby

Gifts from Spirit:
A Skeptic's Path
Dennis Augustine

Hermanos de la Luz:
Brothers of the Light
Ray John de Aragón

Healing Depression:
A Guide to Making Intelligent Choices
about Treating Depression
Catherine Carrigan

Health for Life:
Secrets of Tibetan Ayurveda
Robert Sachs
Foreword by Dr. Lobsang Rapgay

Solitude:
The Art of Living with Yourself
John Selby
October 1998

Inescapable Journey:
A Spiritual Adventure
Claude Saks

In the Presence of My Enemies:
Memoirs of Tibetan Nobleman
Tsipon Shuguba
Sumner Carnahan with Lama Kunga Rinpoche

Message from the Sparrows:
Engaging Consciousness
Taylor Morris

The Search for David:
A Cosmic Journey of Love
George Schwimmer

Strong Brew:
One Man's Prelude to Change
Claude Saks

Tibet:
Enduring Spirit, Exploited Land
Robert Z. Apte and Andrés R. Edwards
Foreword and Poem by His Holiness the Dalai Lama